Cooking with
Frank's® RedHot®
Cayenne Pepper Sauce
Delicious Recipes That Bring the Heat

Rachel Rappaport

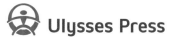 Ulysses Press

Published by
Ulysses Press
P.O. Box 3440
Berkeley, CA 94703
www.ulyssespress.com

ISBN: 978-1-61243-366-0
Library of Congress Catalog Number 2014932297

Printed in the United States by Bang Printing

10 9 8 7 6 5 4 3 2 1

Acquisitions editor: Katherine Furman
Managing editor: Claire Chun
Project editor: Alice Riegert
Editor: Beverly McGuire
Proofreader: Elyce Berrigan-Dunlop
Front cover design: what!design @ whatweb.com
Interior design and layout: what!design @ whatweb.com
Cover photographs: bottle of hot sauce © Jim Lynch, shrimp © Dream79/
    shutterstock.com, buffalo chicken wings © cappi thompson/shutterstock.com;
    chile pepper icon © vip2807/shutterstock.com
Interior photographs: © JudiSwinksPhotography.com
Food stylist: Anna Hartman-Kenzler
Index: Sayre Van Young

Distributed by Publishers Group West

For Matt—with Love and Hot Sauce.

Contents

Introduction

Are you a Frank's® RedHot® lover? If so, you are not alone! People have been loving Frank's® RedHot® Original Cayenne Pepper Sauce since 1920, when the first bottles of cayenne pepper sauce rolled out of the factory. Frank's® RedHot® Original Cayenne Pepper Sauce made history when it was used at the Anchor Bar in Buffalo, New York, in 1964 to make the very first batch of Buffalo hot wings.

Now Frank's® RedHot® Original Cayenne Pepper Sauce is more popular than ever, thanks in no small part to its special recipe, based on the one first made in 1918 by pepper farmer Adam Estilette and partner Jacob Frank, which emphasizes flavor and not just heat.

This cookbook will be your guide to going beyond using Frank's® RedHot® Original Cayenne Pepper Sauce simply as a delicious topping. Wow your friends with Buffalo Chicken Pierogi (page 86), which feature dough filled with chunks of chicken and blue cheese flavored with Frank's® RedHot® Original Cayenne Pepper Sauce. Start your day with Eggs Benedict with Hot Hollandaise (page 15) and end it with Amazing Glazed Turkey Meatloaf (page 62) followed by Sugar and Spice (and Everything Nice) Peach Crumble (page 129). Make a winning spread for the big game with Atomic Wings (page 87), Ultimate Hot Baltimore Crab Dip (page 109), and Mexican Beer Wings with Avocado Ranch Dipping Sauce (page 81). Get ready to use hot sauce in ways you never thought possible.

Kitchen Staples

Half the battle of cooking is being prepared. If your pantry is well stocked, you should be able to make virtually any recipe in this book with little effort. Just add fresh ingredients!

Food Items

Of course, you need to be well stocked with:

- Frank's® RedHot® Original Cayenne Pepper Sauce

- Frank's® RedHot® THICK Cayenne Pepper Sauce

- Frank's® RedHot® Chile N' Lime™ Sauce

- Frank's® RedHot® Sweet Chili Sauce

- Frank's® RedHot® Kickin' BBQ™ Sauce

- Frank's® RedHot® Buffalo Wings Sauce

- Frank's® RedHot® Hot Buffalo Wings Sauce

- Frank's® RedHot® Hot Ketchup Style Sauce™

All of Frank's® RedHot® sauces are available in most supermarkets. If you are having difficulty locating a variety locally, try searching online. Many online stores carry the full range of Frank's products.

The Thick of It

Don't have Frank's® RedHot® THICK Cayenne Pepper Sauce on hand? Try Frank's® RedHot® Hot Ketchup Style Sauce™. It is a little tangier than Frank's® RedHot® THICK but would do in a pinch.

Spices such as cayenne, chipotle, ground mustard, paprika, granulated garlic, dehydrated minced onion, cinnamon, and freshly ground pepper add a ton of flavor to many dishes.

Other flavor boosters include Worcestershire sauce, soy sauce, rice wine vinegar, red wine vinegar, and white vinegar.

Keep a variety of dried and canned beans, canned tomatoes, stocks, and tomato paste on hand to make soup, chilies, and stews in a hurry.

Instant flour, also known as quick mixing flour or gravy flour, is superfine all-purpose flour that is perfect for lightly coating food before frying or for thickening sauces. All-purpose flour, rolled oats, baking powder, and baking soda are all essential ingredients for baking. On the sweet side, an assortment of sugar, including light and dark brown sugar, demerara sugar, confectioner's sugar, and granulated sugar is essential. Honey and agave nectar are also helpful to have on hand when a touch of sweetness is desired.

Ranch Dressing Dry Mix

Ranch dressing is a classic accompaniment to hot wings. Luckily, it is easy to make your own dry mix and keep it on hand for when you need it.

1 cup dry (powdered) buttermilk

2 tablespoons dried parsley

1 tablespoon freeze-dried chives

3 teaspoons dillweed

2 teaspoons dry mustard

1 teaspoon ground paprika

1 teaspoon dehydrated minced onion

½ teaspoon granulated garlic

½ teaspoon onion powder

½ teaspoon fine sea salt

½ teaspoon freshly ground black pepper

In a medium bowl, stir all the ingredients together. When the ingredients are thoroughly combined, store in an airtight container. Will keep up to 1 year at room temperature.

TO MAKE THE DIP

In a medium bowl, thoroughly blend 3 tablespoons of dry mix with 2 cups of sour cream. Let stand 30 minutes before serving to allow the flavors to blend. Refrigerate any leftover dip in an airtight container. Will keep up to 4 days.

TO MAKE THE DRESSING

In a medium bowl, whisk together 1½ tablespoons of the dry mix with ½ cup milk and ⅓ cup mayonnaise. Refrigerate any leftover dressing in an airtight container. Will keep up to 2 days.

Blue Cheese Dressing

If you are more of a blue cheese dressing person, that is easy to make too.

1 cup mayonnaise

¾ cup finely crumbled blue cheese

½ cup buttermilk

2 tablespoons sour cream

2 tablespoons lemon juice

¼ teaspoon Worcestershire sauce

¼ teaspoon kosher salt

½ teaspoon freshly ground black pepper

In a medium bowl, mix all the ingredients together thoroughly. Refrigerate any leftover dressing in an airtight container. Will keep up to 3 days.

Tools and Equipment

Keeping your kitchen stocked with the proper tools and equipment is essential. I keep on hand a variety of wooden and metal spoons, silicone spatulas, measuring cups for both dry and liquid ingredients, measuring spoons, a pair of large tongs, a digital meat thermometer, a citrus reamer, a potato masher, silicone basting brushes, mixing bowls of various sizes, shallow bowls for dredging meat, a smooth-edge can opener, a plastic colander, a large nonstick skillet, a Dutch oven, a 2½-quart saucepan, 12- and 14-inch cast iron skillets, a vegetable peeler, a pepper grinder, knives, and oven mitts.

You don't have to use a lot of fancy appliances to create great food, but for some of the recipes in this book, a slow cooker, blender, mixer with a dough hook attachment, or food processor is quite useful.

Breakfast and Brunch

Nine out of ten Americans eat Frank's® RedHot® Original Cayenne Pepper Sauce on their eggs. Okay, that might not be true, but maybe it should be! Frank's® RedHot® Original Cayenne Pepper Sauce is the perfect condiment to drizzle on your eggs, but that isn't all you can do with it.

Frank's® RedHot® Original Cayenne Pepper Sauce is the perfect ingredient to incorporate into pretty much any breakfast recipe, from decadent eggs Benedict to a fun twist on Bloody Marys to zippy grits. After you try it, you won't want to eat breakfast without it.

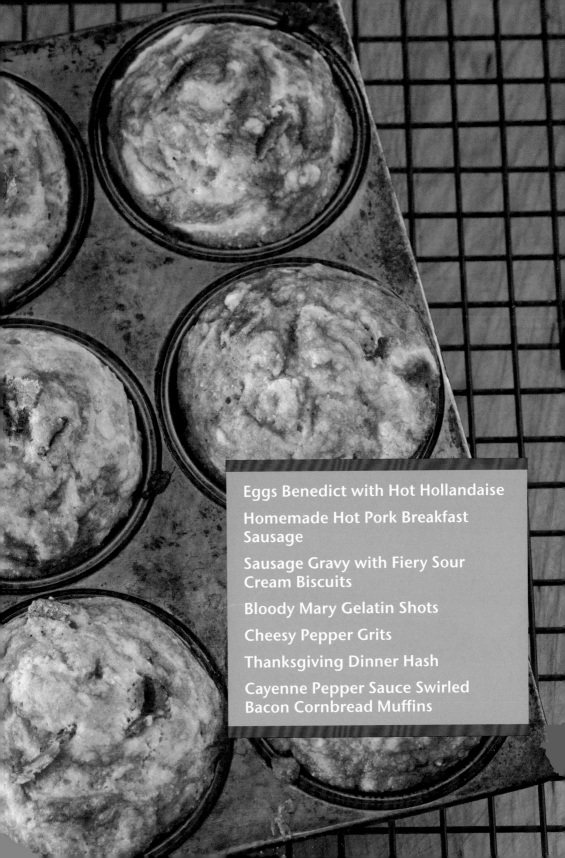

Eggs Benedict with Hot Hollandaise

A fiery version of the classic, this dish is sure to be a hit when served for brunch. You can also try it for breakfast for dinner.

Makes 4 servings (2 muffin halves each)

FOR HOLLANDAISE SAUCE

3 egg yolks

1 tablespoon cold water

3 tablespoons Frank's® RedHot® Original Cayenne Pepper Sauce

½ cup hot melted butter

FOR SERVING

8 eggs, poached

4 English muffins, toasted

8 slices Canadian bacon

1 To make the hollandaise, place the egg yolks, water, and Frank's® RedHot® Original Cayenne Pepper Sauce in a blender and cover. Blend until the mixture is frothy, about 30 seconds. Remove the center insert of the blender cover, and, while the machine is running, stream in the butter very slowly. Continue to blend until a thick sauce forms, about 3 minutes.

2 To poach the eggs bring a pot of water to a boil, add a tablespoon of white vinegar, and crack your eggs, one at a time into the boiling water. Let cook for 6 minutes. Alternatively, you can try using silicone poach pods. Spray the pads with cooking spray, then add the eggs and float them in a small, covered saucepan of boiling water for about 6 minutes.

3 Using 4 plates, place 2 halves of each English muffin on each plate, cut side up. Place the Canadian bacon in a dry skillet and cook over low heat 1–2 minutes or until warmed through. Place a slice of Canadian bacon on each of the 8 English muffin halves on plates. Top each with a poached egg. Drizzle with hollandaise. Serve immediately.

Benedict with a Twist

The B-more: Replace the Canadian bacon with a crab cake or fried oyster.

The Portlandia: Replace the Canadian bacon with sliced avocado and steamed asparagus spears.

The Southern Comfort: Replace the Canadian bacon with country ham and use a split buttermilk biscuit instead of an English muffin.

The Santa Fe: Replace the Canadian bacon with a chorizo patty topped with a roasted green chile.

The Florentine: Replace the Canadian bacon with sautéed spinach topped with a slice of tomato. Use small slices of Italian bread instead of an English muffin.

The Aloha: Add a slice of pineapple and serve on a Hawaiian sweet bread roll instead of an English muffin.

Homemade Hot Pork Breakfast Sausage

Freshly made at home, this breakfast sausage is a revelation to anyone who has only had store-bought sausage. The flavors are bright and spicy; try it on an English muffin with egg for a kicked-up breakfast sandwich.

Makes 8 servings

1½ pounds ground pork

2 tablespoons **Frank's® RedHot® Original Cayenne Pepper Sauce**

2 tablespoons grated fresh onion

½ tablespoon firmly packed dark brown sugar

1½ teaspoons dried sage

1½ teaspoons dried thyme

¼ teaspoon salt

¼ teaspoon dried crushed rosemary

¼ teaspoon freshly ground black pepper

⅛ teaspoon ground cloves

⅛ teaspoon ground nutmeg

⅛ teaspoon ground allspice

1   Place all the ingredients in a medium bowl. Mix thoroughly to combine. Form into 8 small, flat patties, each about 2 inches in diameter. Arrange the patties on a platter and refrigerate 30 minutes to 1 hour.

2   Spray a large skillet lightly with nonstick spray. Over medium heat, cook the patties in the skillet, flipping once halfway through the cooking time, until browned and cooked through, 5–8 minutes total. Remove the cooked patties to paper towel–lined plates to drain. Serve immediately.

Sausage Gravy with Fiery Sour Cream Biscuits

Southern favorite sausage gravy gets a dose of heat, thanks to homemade Frank's® RedHot® Original Cayenne Pepper Sauce sour cream biscuits. Serve with a side of fruit salad for a complete breakfast.

Makes 8 servings

FOR BISCUITS

2¼ cups flour

1 tablespoon baking powder

¼ teaspoon freshly ground black pepper

¼ teaspoon sea salt

1 cup sour cream

½ cup milk

3 tablespoons **Frank's® RedHot® Original Cayenne Pepper Sauce**

FOR SAUSAGE GRAVY

½ tablespoon butter

1 pound bulk pork breakfast sausage

¼ cup flour

½ teaspoon freshly ground black pepper

¼ teaspoon sea salt

2 cups milk

1 Preheat the oven to 425°F. Line a baking sheet with parchment paper. Set aside.

2 To make the biscuits, in a large bowl, whisk together the dry ingredients. Using an electric mixer on medium speed, mix in the sour cream, milk, and Frank's® RedHot® Original Cayenne Pepper Sauce until a smooth dough forms, about 5 minutes.

3 Flour a clean, dry, flat surface. Place the dough on the floured surface and, using a floured rolling pin, roll the dough out to ¾ to 1 inch thick. Use a 3-inch biscuit cutter and cut out biscuits. Arrange the biscuits on the baking sheet, leaving ½ inch of space between the biscuits.

4 Bake for 12–15 minutes or until golden brown. Remove from the baking sheet with a spatula and cool briefly on a wire rack.

5 To make the sausage gravy, while biscuits are baking, melt the butter in a large skillet over medium heat. Add the sausage and cook, breaking up large chunks with the back of a spoon or using a spatula, until browned, about 5–8 minutes. Sprinkle with ¼ cup flour and spices and cook 1 minute more, stirring constantly. Stir in the milk. Cook, stirring continuously, until the mixture thickens, about 5–8 minutes.

6 For each serving, put 1 split biscuit on a plate and pour sausage gravy over it. Serve immediately.

Make It Even More Awesome

Instead of using store-bought pork breakfast sausage, use the Homemade Hot Pork Breakfast Sausage (page 17). Mix the sausage ingredients together, and instead of forming the mixture into patties, follow the instructions here and turn it into sausage gravy.

Bloody Mary Gelatin Shots

Watch out! This jiggly version of the brunch classic cocktail packs a wallop in more ways than one.

Makes 16 (1-ounce) gelatin shots

1 cup tomato-vegetable juice blend, at room temperature

3 tablespoons Frank's® RedHot® Original Cayenne Pepper Sauce

1 tablespoon lemon juice

¼ teaspoon celery salt

5½ teaspoons gelatin powder

¾ cup vodka

FOR GARNISH

celery leaves

prepared horseradish

1   Lightly spray an 8 x 8-inch baking pan with cooking spray. Set aside.

2   In a medium bowl, whisk together the tomato-vegetable juice blend, Frank's® RedHot® Original Cayenne Pepper Sauce, lemon juice, and celery salt. Remove ½ cup of the mixture to a small saucepan.

3   Sprinkle the gelatin over the ½ cup of juice mixture. Allow to sit for 5 minutes. Then, over low heat, warm the juice-gelatin mixture and stir until the gelatin has fully dissolved, about 3 minutes. Pour the juice-gelatin mixture into the medium bowl and whisk into the remaining juice mixture. Whisk in the vodka. Pour into the prepared baking pan and refrigerate 4 hours or until set.

4   To serve, slice the set gelatin mixture into 16 squares. Put each square in a shot glass, top with a celery leaf and a small mound of horseradish, and serve immediately.

Cheesy Pepper Grits

Try this Southern-inspired dish as a side to grilled sausages, fried chicken, or steak. Take care to use stone-ground grits, not instant grits, for best results.

Makes 6 servings

1 poblano pepper, diced

1 medium onion, chopped

3¼ cups chicken stock

¼ cup Frank's® RedHot® Original Cayenne Pepper Sauce

1 cup stone-ground grits

⅓ cup shredded sharp Cheddar cheese

salt to taste

freshly ground black pepper to taste

1 In a small skillet over medium heat, sauté the poblano and onion until the onion is soft, about 5 minutes. Remove from the skillet. Set aside.

2 In a medium pot over medium heat, bring the stock and Frank's® RedHot® Original Cayenne Pepper Sauce to a boil. Add the grits and stir continually for about 10 minutes or until all of the liquid is absorbed. Remove from the heat and stir in the cheese, salt, pepper, and onion mixture. Serve immediately.

Pepper Pointers

Perplexed by peppers? Don't worry, it is easy to handle even the hottest peppers safely. Peppers contain oils that can irritate the skin and other areas of the body. It is worth investing in food-safe gloves (found at most supermarkets) to wear while cutting peppers. Take care not to touch your eyes after handling peppers. Thoroughly wash, using hot, soapy water, all cutlery and cutting boards after cutting up peppers to avoid cross contamination with other food. See page 93 for instructions on how to prepare a pepper for your recipe.

Thanksgiving Dinner Hash

Try this hash on the day after Thanksgiving. It makes great use of Turkey Day leftovers! If you are extra hungry, try topping each portion with a poached or fried egg.

Makes 6 servings

4 strips thick cut bacon

3 Russet potatoes, peeled and diced

1 medium onion, diced

1 pound Brussels sprouts, quartered

4 cups cooked, cubed turkey breast

½ cup **Frank's® RedHot® Original Cayenne Pepper Sauce**

1 In a large skillet over medium heat, cook the bacon until crisp, about 5–8 minutes, flipping the bacon occasionally with tongs so that it browns on both sides. Remove the cooked bacon to paper towel–lined plates to drain. Using kitchen shears, cut the bacon into approximately ¼-inch pieces. Set aside.

2 Drain all but 1–2 tablespoons of bacon grease from the skillet. Return the skillet to the stovetop over medium heat. Add the potatoes, onion, and Brussels sprouts to the remaining bacon grease in the skillet. Sauté 5 minutes, stirring occasionally, then cover. Cook, covered, for 10 minutes more or until the potatoes are fork tender. Add the turkey, crumbled bacon, and Frank's® RedHot® Original Cayenne Pepper Sauce. Stir thoroughly, then cook until warmed through, about 5 minutes. Serve immediately.

Cayenne Pepper Sauce Swirled Bacon Cornbread Muffins

Take cornbread muffins to the next level with the addition of bacon and Frank's® RedHot® THICK Cayenne Pepper Sauce. The perfect spicy start to your day, or try them as a side with chili.

Makes 12 muffins

1 cup cornmeal

1 cup flour

1 teaspoon baking powder

1 teaspoon baking soda

¼ cup sugar

1 egg

1 cup buttermilk

⅓ cup canola oil

⅓ cup cooked, crumbled bacon

12 teaspoons Frank's® RedHot® THICK Cayenne Pepper Sauce

1 Preheat the oven to 400°F. Grease or line with paper liners 1 (12-well) muffin tin.

2 In a medium bowl, whisk together the cornmeal, flour, baking powder, baking soda, and sugar. Beat in the egg, buttermilk, and oil until well combined. Fold in the bacon.

3 Fill each well in the muffin tin ¾ full of batter. Top each muffin with 1 teaspoon Frank's® RedHot® THICK Cayenne Pepper Sauce. Use the tip of a knife to swirl the hot sauce into each muffin.

4 Bake 25 minutes or until the muffins are golden brown and a toothpick inserted in the middle of the center muffin comes out clean. Serve immediately.

Lunch

Poor lunch. So often overlooked because it has none of the pancake and bacon allure of breakfast, nor is it seen as the main meal of the day. It is just lunch, a meal often relegated to frozen meals and boring leftovers.

I say let's take back lunch! Why not make pulled pork overnight in order to have the best afternoon meal ever? Why not pack an exciting, spicy salad to take to the office? Want to spice up a weekend afternoon? Serve a yummy burger instead of boring cold cuts.

Beer-Battered Chicken Sandwiches

Pineapple Pulled Pork

Hot Saucy Joes

Deviled Egg Salad

Spicy Ranch Chicken Salad with Gorgonzola

Buffalo Chicken Burgers

Bison Chili Dogs

Beer-Battered Chicken Sandwiches

Make restaurant-worthy beer-battered sandwiches at home! Thinner cut chicken breast cutlets cook quickly and evenly, so don't be tempted to buy thick chicken breasts instead.

Makes 4 servings

canola oil for frying

¼ cup superfine flour

1 pound thin cut, boneless, skinless chicken breast cutlets

1½ cups IPA beer

3 tablespoons Frank's® RedHot® Original Cayenne Pepper Sauce

1¾ cups flour

FOR SERVING

4 sandwich buns

thinly sliced red onion

lettuce leaves

thinly sliced tomato

additional Frank's® RedHot® Original Cayenne Pepper Sauce or Frank's® RedHot® Hot Ketchup Style Sauce™

1 Heat 1½ inches canola oil in a 12-inch cast iron skillet to 350°F.

2 Meanwhile, place the superfine flour in a shallow bowl. Dredge the chicken breast cutlets in the flour, coating the pieces completely. Set aside.

3 In a medium bowl, whisk together the beer, Frank's® RedHot® Original Cayenne Pepper Sauce, and flour until just combined. Dip each piece of chicken into the mixture and immediately place gently into the hot oil. Fry for about 10 minutes or until golden brown, flipping once using tongs so that the pieces brown evenly.

4 Remove the chicken pieces from the oil and drain on paper towel–lined plates. Serve the chicken immediately on buns topped with onion, lettuce, tomato, and lots of Frank's® RedHot® Original Cayenne Pepper Sauce or Frank's® RedHot® Ketchup Style Hot Sauce™.

Pineapple Pulled Pork

Try this aromatic pulled pork over rice or in a sandwich. If available, try coconut vinegar in place of the apple cider vinegar for an extra taste of the tropics.

Makes 6 servings

2 cups cubed fresh pineapple

1 (2⅓-pound) boneless pork roast

½ tablespoon granulated garlic

½ tablespoon ground ginger

2 tablespoons soy sauce

½ cup Frank's® RedHot® Sweet Chili Sauce

¼ cup apple cider vinegar

1 Place all the ingredients in a 4-quart slow cooker. Cover and cook on low for 8–10 hours or until the pork is easily shredded with a fork. Remove the roast from the slow cooker and shred with forks. Return to the slow cooker, on the warm setting, until ready to serve or serve immediately.

Hot Saucy Joes

Thrill your family's taste buds with this spicy version of the classic sloppy Joe. Temper the heat (if you must!) with a sprinkle of Cheddar cheese on each sandwich.

Makes 8 servings

1 tablespoon olive oil

2 cloves garlic, minced

1 large onion, diced

1 teaspoon ground ancho chile

½ teaspoon red chile flakes

freshly ground black pepper to taste

sea salt to taste

½ cup diced carrot

⅓ pound lean ground beef

⅓ pound ground pork

⅓ pound ground veal

¾ cup tomato paste

½ cup **Frank's® RedHot® Original Cayenne Pepper Sauce**

1 cup apple hard cider

1 tablespoon Worcestershire sauce

1 tablespoon firmly packed light brown sugar

FOR SERVING
8 hamburger or sandwich buns

1 Heat the oil in a large skillet over medium heat. Add the garlic, onion, spices, and carrot and cook, stirring occasionally with a spatula, until fragrant, about 5 minutes. Add meat and sauté until brown, about 5–10 minutes, stirring to break up the meat into small pieces. Add the remaining ingredients. Simmer, uncovered, about 20 minutes, or until the meat is tender and most of the liquid has evaporated.

2 Serve immediately on buns.

Deviled Egg Salad

The devil is in the details in this egg salad. The fresh pepper and celery give it a bit of crunch, and the capers provide the perfect pickle note. Try it on a sandwich or whole wheat crackers.

Makes 6 servings

12 eggs

⅓ cup mayonnaise

3 tablespoons Frank's® RedHot® Original Cayenne Pepper Sauce

2 tablespoons Dijon mustard

⅛ teaspoon whole celery seeds

½ teaspoon ground paprika

¼ teaspoon freshly ground black pepper

⅓ cup diced celery

½ cup diced bell pepper, seeds and veins removed

⅓ cup diced green onion

1½ tablespoons nonpareil capers

1 Place the eggs in a medium pan. Fill the pan with cool water until it is about 1 inch above the eggs. Bring the water to a rapid boil over high heat. When the water comes to a boil, immediately cover the pan and remove it from the heat. Let sit covered for 12 minutes. Remove from the pan and cool on a counter until cool to the touch, about 5 minutes.

2 When the eggs are cool, peel them and slice into eighths. Place in a medium bowl and set aside.

3 Whisk together the mayonnaise, Frank's® RedHot® Original Cayenne Pepper Sauce, mustard, and spices. Set aside.

4 Toss the remaining ingredients with the egg pieces. Drizzle with the sauce mixture and stir to combine well. Serve immediately or refrigerate ½ hour before serving. Refrigerate leftovers.

Spicy Ranch Chicken Salad with Gorgonzola

Leftover roasted, poached, or rotisserie chicken is transformed in this flavor-packed salad. It is awesome in a sandwich, but also try it stuffed into a hollowed-out tomato for a taste sensation.

Makes 6 servings

2½ cups cooked, cubed chicken breast

⅓ cup chopped green onions

¼ cup crumbled Gorgonzola

1 small shallot, minced

1 stalk celery, diced

½ cup mayonnaise

⅓ cup **Frank's® RedHot® Original Cayenne Pepper Sauce**

1½ tablespoons Ranch Dressing Dry Mix (page 10)

1 Place the chicken breast, green onions, Gorgonzola, shallot, and celery in a medium bowl. Toss to mix.

2 In a small bowl, whisk together the mayonnaise, Frank's® RedHot® Original Cayenne Pepper Sauce, and Ranch Dressing Dry Mix. Pour over the chicken mixture and mix until well combined. Refrigerate at least 1 hour prior to serving.

Buffalo Chicken Burgers

These light chicken burgers have all of the flavor and fun of Buffalo wings but without the fuss.

Makes 4 servings

1 pound ground chicken

½ cup bread crumbs

⅓ cup Frank's® RedHot® Buffalo Wings Sauce

2 teaspoons Worcestershire sauce

1 small onion, minced

salt to taste

freshly ground black pepper to taste

FOR SERVING

split crusty rolls

leaf lettuce

tomato slices

1 stalk celery, thinly sliced

Blue Cheese Dressing (page 11)

1 In a medium bowl, mix together the chicken, bread crumbs, Frank's® RedHot® Buffalo Wings Sauce, Worcestershire sauce, onion, salt, and pepper until well combined.

2 Form the mixture into 4 equal patties. With the heel of your hand or a spatula, flatten each patty until it is about ⅓–½ inch thick. Put the patties on a plate and set aside.

3 Spray a large nonstick skillet with cooking spray. Heat 1 minute over medium heat. Add the patties. Cook 4–5 minutes on each side or until the burgers are cooked through and lightly browned.

4 Place the patties on rolls and top with lettuce, tomato, celery, and a dollop of Blue Cheese Dressing. Serve immediately.

Bison Chili Dogs

Chili dogs are an American classic! This version, made with naturally lean American bison, is flavorful without being heavy or greasy. If bison is unavailable, substitute 93% lean ground beef. Use plain tomato sauce and not spaghetti sauce for this recipe.

Makes 8 servings

1 pound ground bison

1 (8 ounce can) tomato sauce

1 cup Frank's® RedHot® Thick Cayenne Pepper Sauce

1 (15 ounce) can dark red kidney beans

1 small onion, chopped

1 clove garlic, minced

1 tablespoon Worcestershire sauce

2 teaspoons hot Mexican chili powder

1 teaspoon ground mustard

½ teaspoon dried oregano leaves

¼ teaspoon whole celery seed

¼ teaspoon ground cumin

FOR SERVING

8 hot dog buns

8 bison or beef hot dogs

Frank's® RedHot® Hot Ketchup Style Sauce™

1 To make the chili, in a large nonstick skillet over medium heat, brown the ground bison for about 5 minutes, stirring occasionally with a spatula to break it up into fine chunks. Add the remaining ingredients. Stir occasionally until most of the liquid has evaporated and everything is cooked through, about 10 minutes.

2 Cook the hot dogs according to your preference. Nestle into buns and top with chili. Serve immediately.

Entrées

This is one of the places where Frank's® RedHot® Original Cayenne Pepper Sauce really shines! Sure, you've had it on a burger or drizzled over chicken, but what if you had fried chicken that not only was marinated in Frank's® RedHot® Original Cayenne Pepper Sauce but also had a ranch-spiced crust? Or stuffed peppers so good that even bell pepper haters will gobble them up?

Or try it in a variety of more exotic uses such as a new take on matzo ball soup that actually puts the hot sauce in the matzo balls or a spicy version of the take-out fave sesame noodles? Get gourmet and make Frank's® RedHot® Original Cayenne Pepper Sauce noodles to serve with a long-cooking bolognaise.

Chili Pie

Try topping this Southwestern favorite with extra fresh peppers, pickled jalapeños, or sour cream. If you serve it directly in the corn chip bag, it is called a walking taco!

Makes 6 servings

2 pounds lean ground beef

5 cloves garlic, chopped

1 large onion, diced

1 jalapeño pepper, minced

3 serrano peppers, minced

¼ cup Frank's® RedHot® Original Cayenne Pepper Sauce

1 (15-ounce) can dark red kidney beans, drained

2 (15-ounce) cans tomatoes with green chiles, drained

1 tablespoon Worcestershire sauce

1 teaspoon dried oregano leaves

2 teaspoons chili powder

1 teaspoon ground ancho chile

1 teaspoon ground chipotle pepper

½ teaspoon ground cumin

3 cups corn chips

⅔ cup chopped white onion

2 cups shredded sharp Cheddar cheese

1 In a Dutch oven or large pot over medium heat, sauté the ground beef, garlic, onion, and peppers until the ground beef is fully browned, about 10 minutes. Add the Frank's® RedHot® Original Cayenne Pepper Sauce, kidney beans, canned tomatoes, Worcestershire sauce, oregano, chili powder, ancho chile, chipotle, and cumin. Reduce the heat to low and simmer until the liquid is mostly evaporated, about 20 minutes.

2 Preheat the oven to 350°F.

3 Cover the bottom of a 9 x 13-inch casserole dish with a single layer of corn chips. Top with the chili. Layer with white onion, then Cheddar cheese. Bake for 15 minutes or until the cheese is melted. Serve immediately.

Catfish Gumbo

A Cajun classic made fresh in your kitchen! For a fun variation, stir in some cooked shrimp or crawfish when you stir in the green onions.

Makes 6 to 8 servings

2½ pounds catfish fillets, cut into bite-sized pieces

2 teaspoons blackened fish seasoning

½ cup Frank's® RedHot® Original Cayenne Pepper Sauce

1 pound Andouille sausage, cut into ¼-inch slices

¼ cup flour

¼ cup canola oil

2 tablespoons Cajun seasoning

½ teaspoon dried oregano leaves

½ teaspoon dried thyme

¼ teaspoon freshly ground black pepper

1 large onion, diced

5 cloves garlic, minced

1½ cups frozen lima beans

1½ cups diced okra

2 jalapeño peppers, diced

1 bell pepper, diced

2 quarts seafood stock, at room temperature

½ pound collard greens, chopped

½ cup chopped green onions

FOR SERVING

4 cups cooked long grain white rice

extra Frank's® RedHot® Original Cayenne Pepper Sauce

1 Place the catfish, blackened fish seasoning, and ½ cup Frank's® RedHot® Original Cayenne Pepper Sauce in a zip-top bag. Toss to coat the fish. Seal the bag and refrigerate 30 minutes.

2 Meanwhile, brown the sausage in a Dutch oven on the stovetop over medium heat. Remove to a plate. Using the same pot in which you browned the sausage, over medium heat, cook the flour, oil, and remaining spices, whisking continuously until the flour starts to brown, about 3 minutes. Stir in the onion, garlic, lima beans, okra, and peppers and sauté until the onion starts to soften and the flour has turned a light brown, 5–10 minutes. Add the stock and whisk until the flour dissolves. Add the

cooked sausage and collards. Over medium heat, cook 20–30 minutes until all the vegetables are tender. Add the catfish and cook another 10 minutes or until the catfish is cooked through. Stir in the green onions.

3 Serve immediately over long grain rice or with Potato Salad for Gumbo (recipe follows) with plenty of Frank's® RedHot® Original Cayenne Pepper Sauce.

Potato Salad for Gumbo

In some areas of rural Louisiana, you might find something strange in the bottom of your bowl of gumbo: potato salad! Smooth and creamy, unlike Southern-style potato salad, it is a cooling treat at the bottom of a spicy dish.

Makes 12 to 15 servings

3 tablespoons powdered crab boil or Chesapeake Bay seasoning

3½ pounds Yukon Gold potatoes, peeled and cubed

⅔ cup minced white onion

1 stalk celery, minced

2 tablespoons chopped jarred pimiento

1 tablespoon minced Italian parsley

½ teaspoon ground paprika

3 tablespoons Creole-style mustard

1¼ cups mayonnaise

sea salt to taste

freshly ground black pepper to taste

1 Bring a large pot of water to a boil. Add the crab boil or seasoning and potatoes. Cook the potatoes until fork tender. Drain and cool.

2 Place the cooled potatoes in a large bowl. Using a potato masher, mash until nearly the texture of mashed potatoes. Stir in the onion, celery, pimiento, and parsley. Set aside.

3 In a small bowl, stir together the paprika, mustard, mayonnaise, salt, and pepper. Pour over the potato mixture. Stir until all the ingredients are evenly distributed. Refrigerate at least 1 hour.

4 When the gumbo is ready to serve, place one large ice cream scoop of the potato salad in the bottom of each serving bowl. Ladle the gumbo over the potato salad. Serve immediately.

Chicken and Veggie– Stuffed Peppers

These peppers might seem plain, but they are packed with flavor, thanks to Frank's® RedHot® Original Cayenne Pepper Sauce, Cheddar cheese, and yummy vegetables.

Makes 4 servings

4 red, green, yellow, or orange bell peppers, or a mix of colors

1 small eggplant, cubed

1 small onion, chopped

2 cups cubed, cooked chicken breast

1 cup fresh or frozen corn kernels

1½ cups shredded extra sharp Cheddar cheese

¾ cup **Frank's® RedHot® Original Cayenne Pepper Sauce**

salt to taste

freshly ground black pepper to taste

1 Preheat the oven to 350°F.

2 Cut the top off each pepper. Discard the tops. Remove the seeds from the peppers. Place the peppers cut side up on a nonstick or lightly oiled baking sheet. Set aside.

In a medium bowl, toss together the remaining ingredients. Fill each pepper with the mixture. Bake until cooked through and the peppers have softened, about 15 minutes. Serve immediately.

Sizzling Sesame Noodles

Try this yummy (and vegan!) riff on take-out favorite sesame noodles topped with fried tofu, toasted sesame seeds, chopped scallions, steamed snow peas, and julienned cucumber and carrot to make it a full meal.

Makes 2 servings

¼ cup soy sauce

1½ tablespoons black sesame oil

1½ tablespoons Frank's® RedHot® Original Cayenne Pepper Sauce

2 tablespoons tahini

1½ tablespoons rice wine vinegar

2 cloves garlic, grated

1 tablespoon grated fresh ginger

1¼ cups soba noodles, cooked, drained, and cooled

1 In a small bowl, whisk together the soy sauce, black sesame oil, Frank's® RedHot® Original Cayenne Pepper Sauce, tahini, rice wine vinegar, garlic, and ginger until smooth. Toss with the noodles and serve immediately.

Blazing Brisket

Slow and low is the name of the game when it comes to brisket. It takes a while, but I promise, it is worth the wait!

Makes 6 servings

FOR SAUCE

1 cup Frank's® RedHot® Original Cayenne Pepper Sauce

⅓ cup firmly packed light brown sugar

⅓ cup amber ale

2 tablespoons Worcestershire sauce

2 tablespoons ground mustard

1 tablespoon honey

1 large onion, minced

2 cloves garlic, minced

FOR BRISKET

1 tablespoon coarse salt

1 teaspoon freshly ground black pepper

2 teaspoons dehydrated minced onion

1 teaspoon granulated garlic

1 (4-pound) beef brisket

1 In a medium bowl, whisk together the sauce ingredients until the sugar dissolves. Remove 1 cup of the sauce and refrigerate it. Reserve the remaining sauce.

2 In a small bowl, mix together the coarse salt, pepper, dehydrated minced onion, and granulated garlic, then rub this mixture onto the brisket on all sides. Place the brisket in a zip-top bag. Pour the reserved sauce on the meat. Seal and refrigerate the brisket 12–18 hours.

3 Prepare the grill according to manufacturer's instructions. Grill the brisket on low heat for 4 hours or until very tender. Remove the brisket from the grill. Wrap in foil and allow to sit for 5 minutes before slicing.

4 While the brisket is resting, pour the refrigerated sauce into a small saucepan. Over low heat, heat until warmed through, about 5 minutes. Remove the brisket from the foil and slice thinly. Serve hot or cold with heated sauce.

Rootin' Tootin' Chili-Topped Baked Potatoes

Try these spicy potatoes topped with cooling sour cream, avocado, and cheese. If you like even more kick, add slices of fresh or pickled jalapeños, a dusting of additional chili powder, spicy hot olives, chopped red onion, and, of course, more Frank's® RedHot® Original Cayenne Pepper Sauce.

Makes 6 servings

6 large Russet potatoes

1 tablespoon canola oil

1 large onion, diced

5 cloves garlic, minced

3 jalapeño peppers, diced

2 cayenne peppers, diced

1 pound 93% lean ground sirloin

2 (15-ounce) cans diced tomatoes, drained

¾ cup tomato paste

½ cup **Frank's® RedHot® Original Cayenne Pepper Sauce**

1 pound frozen black beans

1 pound frozen kidney beans

2 tablespoons chili powder

1 Preheat the oven to 400°F.

2 Pierce each potato in 1 or 2 places with the tip of a knife. Bake for 1 hour or until fully cooked.

3 Heat the oil in a Dutch oven at medium heat. Add the onion, garlic, jalapeños, cayenne peppers, and beef and sauté until the onions are transparent and the beef is nearly fully cooked, about 10 minutes. Add the tomatoes, tomato paste, Frank's® RedHot® Original Cayenne Pepper Sauce, beans, and chili powder and simmer until the mixture is piping hot, about 10–15 minutes.

Slice open the potatoes and top with chili. Serve immediately.

BBQ Chicken Pizza

Pizza night made easy thanks to Frank's® RedHot® Kickin' BBQ™ Sauce and refrigerated pizza dough.

Makes 4 to 6 servings (2 pizzas)

FOR STORE-BOUGHT CRUST

2 (1-pound) balls pizza dough

coarse-grain cornmeal for dusting

FOR HOMEMADE CRUST:

1 cup warm water

¼ teaspoon sugar

2 tablespoons active dry yeast

⅓ cup olive oil

2¾ cups flour

olive oil for greasing bowl

coarse-grain cornmeal for dusting

FOR PIZZA TOPPING

1 cup Frank's® RedHot® Kickin' BBQ™ Sauce, divided, plus more for drizzling

2 cups shredded mozzarella cheese

2 cups shredded, cooked chicken breast

1 cup fresh corn kernels

1 small red onion, halved and thinly sliced

1 Put a large pizza stone or baking sheet on the center rack in the oven. Preheat the oven to 450°F or the temperature specified on the pizza dough package instructions.

TO MAKE THE CRUST USING STORE-BOUGHT DOUGH

Prepare the dough according to package instructions.

TO MAKE THE HOMEMADE PIZZA CRUST

1 Pour warm water into the bowl of a stand mixer or use a large bowl and a hand mixer with a dough hook attachment. Add the sugar and yeast. Stir the mixture until the yeast is dissolved. Stir in the olive oil. Add the flour. Use the dough hook and mix until the dough becomes a smooth, elastic ball, about 5 minutes.

2 Coat the inside of a second large bowl with additional olive oil and place the dough in the bowl, smooth side up. Cover tightly with plastic wrap and place in a cold oven until doubled in size, about 40 minutes. Remove the plastic wrap and use your fist to push down on the center of the dough. Fold the dough in half 4 or 5 times. Turn the dough over, folded side down, cover with plastic wrap, and place on the counter to rise again. Wait until the dough has doubled in size, about 30 minutes.

3 Punch down the dough and transfer to a clean, floured surface. Divide the dough in half and knead each half 4 or 5 times into a ball. Place one of the dough balls back in the oiled bowl and cover with plastic wrap.

4 Place one dough ball on top of the floured surface and pat into a flattened circle about 10 inches in diameter, cover lightly with plastic wrap, and let rest 5 minutes. Then use a floured rolling pin to flatten and push the dough evenly out from the center until it measures about 7 to 8 inches in diameter and is about ¼ inch thick. Lift the dough off the surface and center it on top of your fists. Rotate and stretch the dough, moving your fists until they are 6 to 8 inches apart and the dough is several inches larger. Then place your fists under the inside of the outer edge, and continue to stretch the dough until it reaches about 12 inches in diameter. The dough will drape down over your forearms. Start over if the dough tears or is see-through.

TO ASSEMBLE AND BAKE THE PIZZAS

1 Sprinkle a pizza peel lightly with cornmeal. Gently lay the stretched-out homemade dough from half the recipe or the rolled-out dough from one ball of store-bought pizza dough on the pizza peel. Spread the dough with Frank's® RedHot® Kickin' BBQ™ Sauce, leaving a ½-inch border around the outer edge of the pizza. Cover the pizza with half the cheese, chicken, corn, and red onion. Drizzle the pizza with more Frank's® sauce.

2 Sprinkle a little cornmeal on the hot pizza stone or baking sheet. Gently slide unbaked pizza off the pizza peel and onto the stone or baking sheet. Bake the pizza for 10 minutes or until the crust is fully cooked and the cheese is melted. When the pizza is done, use pizza peel to remove it from the oven. Slide the pizza off pizza peel onto a flat surface to cool.

3 While the first pizza is cooling, repeat the entire process to make the second pizza. Serve immediately.

Saucy Southern Sausage Bean Soup

This soup couldn't be easier, cheaper, or more crowd pleasing if it tried! Serve it with extra Frank's® RedHot® Original Cayenne Pepper Sauce on the side so people can sauce it up as much as they like.

Makes about 10 servings

1 pound dried navy beans

1 teaspoon ground smoked paprika

1 teaspoon ground mustard

½ teaspoon salt

½ teaspoon freshly ground black pepper

1 large onion, diced

1 stalk celery, diced

1 parsnip, diced

1 carrot, diced

8 cups chicken stock

¼ cup Frank's® RedHot® Original Cayenne Pepper Sauce

2 cups frozen diced okra

1½ cups smoked turkey sausage

1 The night before you want to serve the dish, place the navy beans in a 4-quart slow cooker. Fill it with water. Cover and allow the beans to soak overnight.

2 The following morning, drain the navy beans, then return them to the slow cooker.

3 Add the paprika, mustard, salt, pepper, onion, celery, parsnip, carrot, stock, and Frank's® RedHot® Original Cayenne Pepper Sauce to the slow cooker. Cook on low for 8 hours.

4 After 8 hours, stir in the okra and sausage. Continue to cook on low for 10 minutes or until the okra is hot and fully defrosted. Serve immediately.

Bolognese Alla Diavola Pappardelle

A classic Italian sauce paired with hot sauce–spiked pasta? Sounds crazy, but trust me, it is amazing. Somehow the addition of the hot sauce makes the pasta silky smooth and incredibly easy to work with. It is the perfect light, tasty, fresh foil for a rich, meaty sauce.

Makes 6 to 8 servings

FOR SAUCE

1 tablespoon olive oil

1 large onion, diced

2 carrots, diced

1 pound hot Italian sausage

1 pound 90% lean ground beef

1 tablespoon red pepper flakes

¼ teaspoon ground nutmeg

½ cup whole milk

½ cup dry red wine

3½ cups canned crushed tomatoes

1 (15 ounce can) diced tomatoes

freshly ground black pepper to taste

sea salt to taste

FOR PASTA

2 pounds flour

10 eggs

3 tablespoons **Frank's® RedHot® Original Cayenne Pepper Sauce**

TO MAKE THE SAUCE

1 Heat the olive oil in a Dutch oven or tall-sided skillet over medium heat. Cook the onion and carrots until the onions are translucent and soft, stirring occasionally, about 5–8 minutes. Add the sausage and ground beef and cook, stirring occasionally and breaking up any large chunks, until the meat is browned, about 8–10 minutes.

2 Add the spices and milk. Simmer, stirring occasionally, until the milk has cooked down and the meat looks dry, about 20 minutes. Add the wine and simmer, stirring occasionally, until the wine has cooked down and the meat looks dry, about 20 minutes. Add the tomatoes and simmer for

at least 1½ hours and up to 3½ hours, adding small amounts of water occasionally if the mixture looks dry. When the sauce is done, add salt and pepper to taste.

TO MAKE THE PASTA

1 Place the ingredients in a large bowl. Start mixing either by hand or with a mixer with a dough hook until a dough forms. Remove the dough to a lightly floured cutting board and knead, sprinkling on small amounts of flour as necessary, until the dough is smooth and no longer sticky.

2 Divide the dough into 12 pieces and follow the manufacturer's instructions for your pasta machine to create sheets of pasta. Gently fold the sheets in half and slice them into 1-inch-wide strips.

3 Bring a large pot of salted water to a boil. Cook the pasta until al dente, 2–3 minutes.

4 Drain the pasta and then serve immediately topped with the sauce. Store the pasta and sauce leftovers separately.

Amazing Glazed Turkey Meatloaf

Two kinds of Frank's® RedHot® Original Cayenne Pepper Sauce pep up this simple, satisfying turkey meatloaf. Try the leftovers on a sandwich spread with even more Frank's® RedHot® Original Cayenne Pepper Sauce!

Makes 6 servings

2 pounds ground turkey

¼ cup Frank's® RedHot® Original Cayenne Pepper Sauce

1 egg, beaten

⅔ cup bread crumbs

2 tablespoons dehydrated minced onion

1 teaspoon granulated garlic

salt to taste

freshly ground black pepper to taste

½ cup Frank's® RedHot® THICK Cayenne Pepper Sauce

1 Preheat the oven to 400°F.

2 In a large bowl, mix together the turkey, Frank's® RedHot® Original Cayenne Pepper Sauce, egg, bread crumbs, and spices until well combined. Form into a loaf. Place in a standard (8½ x 4½-inch) loaf pan. Brush with Frank's® RedHot® THICK Cayenne Pepper Sauce.

3 Bake for 40 minutes or until fully cooked. Let stand on the counter for 5 minutes, then slice and serve.

Hot Ranch Fried Chicken

Be prepared to eat the best fried chicken of your life. The chicken is bursting with Frank's® RedHot® Original Cayenne Pepper Sauce flavor, and the delicate, crisp crust has the wonderful flavor of ranch.

Makes 4 to 6 servings

1 (7-pound) fryer chicken, cut into pieces

1 cup milk

1 cup Frank's® RedHot® Original Cayenne Pepper Sauce

6 tablespoons Ranch Dressing Dry Mix (page 10)

2 cups flour

salt to taste

freshly ground black pepper to taste

canola oil for frying

1 Place the chicken pieces in a zip-top bag. Add the milk and Frank's® RedHot® Original Cayenne Pepper Sauce to the bag, seal it, and shake gently to coat the chicken pieces. Refrigerate overnight.

2 In a medium bowl, whisk together the Ranch Dressing Dry Mix, flour, salt, and pepper. Set aside.

3 Drain the chicken in a colander. Discard the marinade. Dredge the chicken pieces in the flour mixture, coating the pieces on all sides, and arrange the coated pieces on a platter.

4 After coating the chicken in the flour mixture, heat 1 inch oil in a 14-inch cast iron skillet to 350°F. Fry the chicken, in batches, until fully cooked and golden brown, about 15 minutes. Turn with tongs occasionally during cooking if the chicken pieces are not fully submerged in oil so that they brown on all sides. Drain the chicken pieces on paper towel–lined plates or on a baking rack placed over a baking sheet to catch drips. Serve immediately.

Tex-Mex Pork Chili

Serve this chili with Cayenne Pepper Sauce Swirled Bacon Cornbread Muffins (page 25) and plenty of sour cream, chopped onions, pickled jalapeños, lime wedges, and shredded sharp Cheddar cheese.

Makes 8 servings

1 (2½-pound) boneless pork roast, cubed

2 cloves garlic, minced

1 carrot, diced

1 fresh ancho chile, diced

½ teaspoon ground hot paprika

½ teaspoon ground ancho chile

2 tablespoons hot New Mexican chili powder

½ cup Frank's® RedHot® Chile N' Lime™ Hot Sauce

2 (15-ounce) cans diced tomatoes with green chiles, drained

2 (15-ounce) cans Mexican-style chili hot beans (not drained)

1 In a large nonstick skillet over medium heat, brown the pork pieces, turning with a spatula so that all sides get browned, about 5 minutes total. Add to a 4-quart slow cooker. Add the remaining ingredients to the pork and stir. Cook on low for 8–10 hours. Stir and serve immediately.

Pickled Jalapeños

A favorite topping for chili, an original ingredient in nachos, and the perfect addition to tacos, pickled jalapeños have so many uses! Here I provide one recipe with two outcomes: one makes a canned pickle that can be stored up to one year, and the second makes a fresh refrigerated pickle that can last up to 6 weeks. I bet you'll eat them all before then, though!

Makes about 4 pints

1 pound whole jalapeño peppers

¼ cup black peppercorns

2½ teaspoons dill seeds

2 tablespoons yellow mustard seeds

4 cloves garlic, peeled

8 fresh bay leaves

4 cups water

4 cups white vinegar

¼ cup pickling salt

1 Slice the jalapeños in half. Cut the tops off any very large jalapeños to allow them to fit in the jars. Set aside.

2 Divide the peppercorns, dill seeds, mustard seeds, garlic, and bay leaves evenly between 4 canning pint jars. Fill each jar with as many jalapeños as can fit, leaving at least ¼ inch room at the top of each jar. Set aside.

3 In a medium saucepan, bring the water, vinegar, and salt to a boil. Stir to dissolve the salt. Ladle the hot mixture into the jars, filling each one to ¼ inch from the top.

TO PRESERVE FOR FUTURE USE (UP TO 1 YEAR):

1 Fill a canning pot with water and bring it to a boil.

2 Soften the discs of four 2-part canning lids in hot water for 10 minutes. Place 1 disc on each jar. Add the ring part of a lid to each jar and close until just finger tight (don't force it closed). Set the jars aside. Place the jars on a canning rack and place the rack in the boiling water in the canning pot. Jars should be completely covered with water. Boil the jars for 10 minutes at a full boil. Remove the jars using jar tongs and allow to cool completely. For each jar, remove the ring part of the lid and check the disc seal. Refrigerate any jars that did not seal. Store sealed jars in a cool, dark place up to 1 year.

3 After canning, wait 1 week prior to serving to give the flavors time to blend.

IF USING IMMEDIATELY (UP TO 6 WEEKS):

1 Close the jars. Allow them to cool completely. Store in the refrigerator. Wait 1 week prior to serving to give the flavors time to blend. Consume all the peppers within 6 weeks.

Hot Chicken Cobb Salad

This is a spicy version of the salad invented at the Brown Derby in the 1930s. Try using leftover rotisserie chicken and cooking the bacon and eggs the day before you want to serve them to make this super quick to pull together on a week night.

Makes 4 servings

FOR SALAD

1 head Boston lettuce, chopped

1 bunch watercress, chopped

1 head romaine, chopped

2 tomatoes, cubed

5 strips bacon, cooked and cut into ½-inch pieces

1 pound cooked, cubed chicken breast

4 hard-boiled eggs, diced

2 avocados, peeled, pitted, and cubed

½ cup crumbled Roquefort cheese

2 tablespoons chopped chives

FOR DRESSING

¼ cup red wine vinegar

⅔ cup olive oil

3 tablespoons Frank's® RedHot® Original Cayenne Pepper Sauce

½ teaspoon Dijon mustard

1 clove garlic, finely minced

salt to taste

freshly ground black pepper to taste

1 Gently toss together the salad ingredients in a large bowl. Set aside.

2 Place all of the salad dressing ingredients in a dressing shaker or lidded jar. Shake until well combined.

3 Drizzle the salad dressing over the salad and toss gently. Serve immediately.

Shuffle Off to Buffalo Pie

Garlic-infused Gorgonzola potatoes top a rich, creamy chicken mixture spiced with Frank's® RedHot® Original Cayenne Pepper Sauce in this take on shepherd's pie.

Makes 8 to 10 servings

FOR POTATO LAYER

2 pounds Russet potatoes, peeled and cubed

4 large cloves garlic, peeled

⅓ cup milk

1 tablespoon butter

⅔ cup crumbled Gorgonzola

FOR CHICKEN LAYER

1 tablespoon butter

1 large onion, diced

2 stalks celery, diced

1½ cups shredded carrots

4 cups cooked, cubed chicken breast

⅔ cup milk

⅔ cup Frank's® RedHot® THICK Cayenne Pepper Sauce

¾ cup frozen corn

¼ cup instant flour

salt to taste

freshly ground black pepper to taste

1 Preheat the oven to 350°F.

2 Bring a large pot of water to a boil. Add the potatoes and garlic and boil until the potatoes are fork tender, about 10 minutes. Drain the garlic and potatoes and return them to the pot. Add the milk, butter, and Gorgonzola. Mash with a potato masher until smooth. Set aside.

3 Meanwhile, in a large skillet over medium heat, melt the butter. Add the onion, celery, and carrots and cook, stirring occasionally, until the onion is softened, about 5 minutes. Add the chicken, milk, Frank's® RedHot® THICK Cayenne Pepper Sauce, and corn. Cook for 5 minutes, stirring occasionally. Sprinkle with instant flour, salt, and pepper. Continue to cook, stirring occasionally, until the mixture thickens and there is almost no visible liquid remaining.

4 Lightly butter a 9 x 13-inch baking dish. Pour the chicken mixture into the baking dish and spread evenly. Spread the potato mixture over the chicken. Bake for 40 minutes or until bubbly and warmed through. Serve immediately.

Red Hot Sopes with Slow Cooker Carnitas

Sopes are a treat that originated in central and southern Mexico but have now spread all over. They can be topped with a variety of meats, but my particular favorite is carnitas. They are traditionally made by slow-cooking on the grill, but I simplified the process by using a slow cooker and then broiling them to crisp the meat.

Makes 4 servings

FOR CARNITAS

1 large onion, sliced

1 teaspoon garlic powder

1 teaspoon dehydrated minced onion

1 (2½-pound) boneless pork roast

1 teaspoon ground ancho chile

1 teaspoon ground cayenne pepper

½ teaspoon dried oregano

FOR SOPES

1 cup masa harina

½ cup Frank's® RedHot® Original Cayenne Pepper Sauce

½ cup water

canola oil for frying

FOR SERVING

1 cup shredded lettuce

½ cup crema (Mexican sour cream)

1 To make the carnitas, line the bottom of a 4-quart slow cooker insert with onion slices. In a small bowl, whisk together the garlic powder and dehydrated minced onion. Rub onto all sides of the pork roast. Place the pork roast in the slow cooker over the onions. Cook on low for 8 hours.

2 Remove the pork to a cutting board. Use 2 forks to shred the meat. Add it back to the slow cooker. Toss to coat in liquid.

3 Line a baking sheet with foil. Remove the pork from the slow cooker. Arrange the pork in a single layer over the foil. Broil on high for 5–10 minutes or until crisped around the edges. Cover to keep warm if needed.

4 After the carnitas have cooked for about 7 hours, begin to prepare the sopes. Place the masa harina, Frank's® RedHot® Original Cayenne Pepper Sauce, and water in a large bowl and hand mix until a crumbly dough forms. Form the dough into 8 equal-sized balls.

5 Place 4 balls, about 2 inches apart, between two 1½-foot-long sheets of waxed paper. Using the heel of your hand, press a dough ball down until it forms a flattened circle about ¼ inch thick and 2½ to 3 inches in diameter. Pinch the edges of the dough to create a small ridge ¼ inch high. Repeat for remaining dough balls.

6 Fill a large skillet with ½ inch canola oil. Heat the oil to about 350°F. Add the sopes, flat side down, and fry until brown, about 2 minutes. Drain on paper towel–lined plates. Repeat for the remaining sopes.

7 Top each sope with a small amount of carnitas, then top with shredded lettuce and a drizzle of crema. Serve immediately.

Roasted Buffalo Tofu and Cabbage

Try this hearty vegan dish over hot cooked rice or quinoa or serve as is. Feel like a change? Try using broccoli heads or cauliflower wedges instead of the cabbage.

Makes 4 servings

1½ cups extra firm tofu

1 cup Frank's® RedHot® Hot Buffalo Wings Sauce

sea salt to taste

freshly ground black pepper to taste

1 teaspoon canola oil

FOR CABBAGE

½ head cabbage, cut into 4 wedges

½ large onion, sliced

½ cup Frank's® RedHot® Hot Buffalo Wings Sauce

2 tablespoons canola oil

½ tablespoon granulated garlic

¼ teaspoon whole celery seed

½ teaspoon freshly ground black pepper

1 tablespoon toasted sesame seeds

1 Drain the tofu in a colander and wrap it in paper towels or a tea towel. Place on a rimmed baking sheet. Place a cutting board on top of the tofu. Arrange 4–6 large, heavy cans on top of the baking sheet over the tofu. Allow to press 1 hour. Remove the cans and cutting board, unwrap the tofu, and cut it into ½-inch cubes. Place in a medium bowl and toss with Frank's® RedHot® Hot Buffalo Wings Sauce, spices, and canola oil. Allow to soak 1 hour.

2 Preheat the oven to 350°F.

3 Line 2 baking sheets with parchment paper. Drain the tofu and place in a single layer on 1 baking sheet. Arrange the cabbage, point side up, on the second baking sheet. Sprinkle the onion over the cabbage.

4 In a small bowl, whisk together the ½ cup of Frank's® RedHot® Hot Buffalo Wings Sauce, canola oil, garlic, celery seed, and pepper. Pour over the cabbage and onion.

5 Place the baking sheets with the tofu and cabbage in the oven. Bake 60 minutes, flipping the tofu once, or until the tofu is crisp and the cabbage is fork tender. Sprinkle the cabbage with sesame seeds. Serve immediately.

Hot-zah Ball Soup

This spicy version of matzo ball soup will have you asking for more! It is simple to make but is a bit time consuming. Luckily, this soup, flavored with dried chiles in the base, fresh chiles in the soup, and Frank's® RedHot® Original Cayenne Pepper Sauce in the matzo balls, is well worth the effort.

Makes 8 to 10 servings

FOR BASE
4 cloves garlic, chopped

4 parsnips, halved

4 carrots, halved

4 stalks celery, halved

2 large onions, quartered

1 bunch fresh parsley

2 gaujillo chile peppers

1 (3–4 pound) chicken, cut into pieces, skin and fat removed and reserved

2 quarts chicken stock

FOR MATZO BALLS
¼ cup diced onion

¾ cup water

¼ cup Frank's® RedHot® Original Cayenne Pepper Sauce

1 cup matzo meal

1 egg, beaten

2 tablespoons minced Italian parsley

½ teaspoon white pepper

salt for water

FOR SOUP
3 carrots, cut into coins

3 parsnips, cut into coins

3 stalks celery, sliced

3 jalapeño peppers, sliced

1 large onion, diced

1½ cups chicken stock (if needed)

sea salt to taste

freshly ground black pepper to taste

TO MAKE THE BASE

1 Place all of the base ingredients in an 8- or 10-quart stockpot. Bring to a boil, then reduce to low and simmer, partially covered, for 1 hour or until the chicken is fully cooked. Skim and discard any surface foam. Remove

the chicken from the base. Remove all meat from the bones and cut into bite-sized pieces. Set aside. Discard bones.

TO MAKE THE MATZO BALLS

1 Heat a sauté pan over medium heat and add the reserved chicken skin and fat and the ¼ cup diced onion. Cook over medium heat until all the fat is rendered, about 20 minutes. The onion and skin should be very crisp and well browned. Strain the rendered fat through a colander into a medium heat-safe bowl or liquid measuring cup. Measure out ¼ cup of rendered fat. Set aside. Refrigerate the leftover fat for another use or discard.

2 Bring the water, salt, and Frank's® RedHot® Original Cayenne Pepper Sauce to a boil. Pour over the matzo meal in a large bowl. Stir in the rendered fat, egg, parsley, and pepper until thoroughly blended. Refrigerate 30 minutes to 1 hour.

TO MAKE THE SOUP

1 Strain the base broth through a fine strainer into another large pot, pressing the solids to release any liquid. Discard solids. If a very clear broth is desired, strain again through cheesecloth. Add the reserved chicken, carrots, parsnips, celery, jalapeño peppers, and onion. Stir. If the mixture isn't well covered with stock, add the additional 1½ cups chicken stock. Add salt and pepper to taste. Return the broth to a boil, then reduce the heat to low and simmer uncovered for 30 minutes or until vegetables are fork tender.

2 Meanwhile, remove the matzo meal mixture from the refrigerator and, using lightly oiled hands, roll into 1-inch balls. Bring salted water to a boil in a medium stockpot. Drop the matzo balls into the water and cook 15 minutes or until done. Matzo balls will float to the surface when fully cooked. Remove with a slotted spoon.

TO SERVE

1 Ladle the soup into bowls, then top with the matzo balls. Serve immediately. Store leftover soup and matzo balls separately in the refrigerator.

Pro Tips

• Guajillo chiles are dried mirasol chiles. Look for them in Mexican grocery stores or the international section of the supermarket. If you can't find them, use dried Anaheim chile peppers (also known as New Mexican chile peppers or *chile seco del norte*).

• Matzo meal is ground matzo. Make your own matzo meal by pulsing sheets of matzo in a food processor, or buy it premade at the supermarket. Look for it near kosher or international foods. It is available year round but is often on sale at a great discount near Passover.

Appetizers and Snacks

Okay, I bet tons of you flipped directly to this chapter. Wings!! Give me wings!! And wings you shall have. Not only the classic Buffalo wing Frank's® RedHot® Original Cayenne Pepper Sauce made famous but also extra hot wings, baked wings, Mexican Beer Wings, and even tangy Asian-inspired wings. Wings galore.

Want to move beyond wings? Impress your friends by serving Buffalo-style oysters...in the shell. Or whip up some tangy Buffalo Chicken Pierogi. These are just a few ways that you can take your appetizers to the next level.

Classic Buffalo Wings

Serve with plenty of napkins, celery sticks, and blue cheese or ranch dressing. Making wings for a crowd? Double or triple the recipe and keep the cooked wings warm on a platter in a 200°F oven.

Makes 4 servings

24 chicken wings, separated into drums and flats

1½ tablespoons instant flour

salt to taste

freshly ground black pepper to taste

canola oil for frying

1½ cups Frank's® RedHot® Buffalo Wings Sauce

1 In a large bowl, toss the wings with flour, salt, and pepper to taste. Set aside.

2 In a 12-inch skillet, heat 2 inches of canola oil to 350°F. Add half of the wings to the skillet. Fry until golden brown on both sides, about 10 minutes, turning as needed with tongs to make sure pieces are evenly browned. Remove to a large bowl and toss with the sauce. Repeat with the remaining wings. Toss again. Serve immediately.

Baked Classic Buffalo Wings

A walk on the lighter side, these wings have all of the flavor of the classic fried wings but less fat. Try them dipped in blue cheese or ranch dressing or simply tossed with additional Frank's® RedHot® Hot Buffalo Wings Sauce.

Makes 4 servings

24 chicken wings, separated into flats and drums

1 cup Frank's® RedHot® Hot Buffalo Wings Sauce

½ teaspoon ground cayenne pepper

freshly ground black pepper to taste

1 tablespoon canola oil plus oil to grease the pan

1 Place the wings in a zip-top bag. Set aside.

2 In a small bowl, whisk together Frank's® RedHot® Hot Buffalo Wings Sauce and the spices. Pour into the bag over the wings. Refrigerate for 30 minutes.

3 Preheat the oven to 400°F. Line a baking sheet with foil. Lightly oil the foil.

4 Drain the wings in a colander and toss them in a large bowl with 1 tablespoon oil. Arrange in a single layer on the baking sheet and bake for 40 minutes or until fully cooked and crispy. Serve immediately.

Oven-Baked Crispy Catfish Nuggets

These surprisingly light catfish nuggets are a delightful alternative to their chicken counterparts. Try them dipped in Hot and Spicy Cocktail Sauce (page 107).

Makes 6 servings

2 pounds catfish fillets, cut into bite-sized pieces

1½ cups buttermilk

½ cup Frank's® RedHot® Original Cayenne Pepper Sauce

1 teaspoon Dijon mustard

1 jalapeño pepper, diced

¼ teaspoon freshly ground black pepper

2 cups bread crumbs

2 teaspoons chili powder

2 teaspoons ground chipotle pepper

1 teaspoon ground paprika

2 teaspoons ground ancho chile

1 Place the catfish, buttermilk, Frank's® RedHot® Original Cayenne Pepper Sauce, mustard, jalapeño, and black pepper in a zip-top plastic bag or marinating container. Refrigerate for at least 30 minutes and up to 1 hour. Drain the catfish and discard the marinade.

2 Preheat the oven to 350°F.

3 In a shallow bowl, mix together the bread crumbs and remaining spices. Dip each nugget in the crumbs to coat and arrange in a single layer on a parchment paper–lined baking sheet. Bake 20 minutes or until fully cooked. Serve immediately.

Buffalo Fried Oysters

A stunning appetizer, Buffalo Fried Oysters are a unique twist to the classic Buffalo wing. If oyster shells are not available, serve in small, shallow ramekins or Chinese soup spoons.

Makes 8 to 10 servings

2 cups shucked, raw "frying size" oysters

½ cup Frank's® RedHot® Original Cayenne Pepper Sauce, divided for use

2 eggs, beaten

⅔ cup flour

⅔ cup bread crumbs

1 teaspoon ground paprika

¼ teaspoon salt

¼ teaspoon freshly ground black pepper

canola oil for frying

2 tablespoons butter, melted

1 teaspoon agave nectar

½ cup Blue Cheese Dressing (page 11)

FOR SERVING
15–20 oyster shell halves

1 Pour the oysters into a small bowl. Add ¼ cup Frank's® RedHot® Original Cayenne Pepper Sauce. Refrigerate for 20 minutes.

2 Meanwhile, pour the eggs, flour, and bread crumbs into 3 separate shallow bowls. Stir the spices into the bread crumbs. Set aside.

3 Heat about ½ inch oil in a large, shallow skillet over medium-high heat. Dredge each oyster in the flour, then the eggs, then the seasoned bread crumbs, taking care to thoroughly coat the oyster on all sides. Gently place the oysters one at a time in the hot oil. Cook until golden on all sides, about 2 minutes. Remove to a paper towel–lined plate to drain. Remove the drained oysters to a shallow medium bowl.

4 Whisk the remaining Frank's® RedHot® Original Cayenne Pepper Sauce, butter, and agave nectar together in a small bowl. Drizzle over the oysters. Gently toss to coat.

5 Place each oyster on a shell and garnish with a dollop of Blue Cheese Dressing. Serve immediately.

General Mattso's Shrimp

This riff on a classic Hong Kong dish is as hot as it is tasty! Serve it on skewers (mini-skewers work great) or on toothpicks for easy eating. Serve any leftover sauce on the side for dipping.

Makes 8 to 10 servings

1 pound large (31–35 count) shrimp, peeled and deveined

sea salt to taste

freshly ground black pepper to taste

FOR SAUCE

1 teaspoon sesame oil

1 teaspoon canola oil

2 teaspoons minced ginger

2 teaspoons minced garlic

¼ cup minced onion

1 jalapeño pepper, seeds and veins removed, minced

¼ cup **Frank's® RedHot® Original Cayenne Pepper Sauce**

2 tablespoons hoisin sauce

1 tablespoon honey

1 tablespoon chile garlic sauce

2 teaspoons Worcestershire sauce

1 Prepare grill according to the manufacturer's instructions. Preheat the grill to medium heat. While the grill is preheating, skewer the shrimp with bamboo skewers. Sprinkle with salt and pepper. Grill the shrimp, turning once, until fully cooked, 2–4 minutes. Remove from the grill.

TO MAKE THE SAUCE

1 Heat the sesame oil and canola oil in a small skillet over medium heat. Add the ginger, garlic, onion, and jalapeño to the oil and sauté until softened and fragrant, about 3–5 minutes. Remove from the heat and stir in the remaining ingredients until well distributed.

2 Brush the sauce on both sides of the shrimp. Serve immediately, with or without the skewers.

Mexican Beer Wings with Avocado Ranch Dipping Sauce

Paired with cooling avocado ranch dipping sauce, these piquant wings are sure to delight chile lovers.

Makes 4 servings

FOR WINGS

24 chicken wings, separated into flats and drums

½ cup lime juice

1 cup Frank's® RedHot® Chile N' Lime™ Hot Sauce

1 cup IPA beer

1 small red onion, chopped

freshly ground black pepper to taste

1 tablespoon oil, plus oil to grease the pan

FOR DIPPING SAUCE

1 avocado, peeled and pitted

2 tablespoons lime juice

1 teaspoon garlic powder

2 cups sour cream

3 tablespoons Ranch Dressing Dry Mix (page 10)

1 Place the wings in a zip-top bag. Set aside.

2 In a small bowl, whisk together the lime juice, Frank's® RedHot® Chile N' Lime™ Hot Sauce, beer, onion, and pepper. Pour over the wings in the bag. Refrigerate for 30 minutes.

3 Preheat the oven to 400°F. Line a baking sheet with foil. Lightly oil the foil.

4 Drain the wings in a colander and toss them with 1 tablespoon oil in a large bowl. Arrange in a single layer and bake for 40 minutes or until fully cooked and crispy. Serve immediately with Avocado Ranch Dipping Sauce on the side.

TO MAKE THE DIPPING SAUCE

1 Place the avocado in a medium bowl. Mash with a potato masher until fairly smooth. Stir in remaining ingredients until evenly distributed. Refrigerate until ready to use. Refrigerate leftovers.

Game Day Popcorn Munch

Wow your friends and neighbors on game day with this spicy, zesty popcorn treat. Use air-popped popcorn for a lighter snack.

Makes 8 to 10 servings

3 quarts popped plain popcorn

1 cup roasted, lightly salted peanuts

½ teaspoon lime zest

2 tablespoons butter, melted

¼ teaspoon mustard powder

1½ tablespoons **Frank's® RedHot® Original Cayenne Pepper Sauce**

2 teaspoons lime juice

salt to taste (optional)

1 Place the popcorn and peanuts in a large bowl. Sprinkle with lime zest. Set aside.

2 In a small bowl, whisk together the butter, mustard powder, Frank's® RedHot® Original Cayenne Pepper Sauce, and lime juice. Drizzle over the popcorn mixture and toss. Lightly salt, if desired. Toss again and serve immediately.

Party Mix

Frank's® RedHot® Original Cayenne Pepper Sauce brings the classic party mix to a whole new level! Customize it by swapping out the mixed nuts for pumpkin or sunflower seeds.

Makes about 24 servings

¼ cup melted butter

2 teaspoons **Frank's® RedHot® Original Cayenne Pepper Sauce**

1 teaspoon garlic powder

1 teaspoon onion powder

1 teaspoon ground paprika

1 teaspoon dried parsley

1 teaspoon dillweed

½ teaspoon kosher salt

1 teaspoon ground chipotle pepper

2 cups crispy corn cereal squares

2 cups crispy wheat cereal squares

2 cups crispy rice cereal squares

1 cup fish-shaped Cheddar crackers

1 cup mini pretzels

1 cup roasted, unsalted mixed nuts

1 Preheat the oven to 250°F.

2 In a large bowl, whisk together the butter, Frank's® RedHot® Original Cayenne Pepper Sauce, garlic powder, onion powder, paprika, parsley, dillweed, salt, and ground chipotle. Add the remaining ingredients and gently toss to coat.

3 Pour the mixture onto a large baking sheet in a single layer and bake for 1 hour, stirring every 15 minutes. Spread on paper towel–lined plates in a single layer and allow to cool fully before serving. Store leftovers in an airtight container.

Buffalo Chicken Pierogi

Frank's® RedHot® Original Cayenne Pepper Sauce flavors dough envelopes filled with savory chicken and blue cheese to form a pierogi that is sure to become a new favorite. Try them dipped in sour cream spiked with a bit of Frank's® RedHot® THICK Cayenne Pepper Sauce.

Makes 25 to 30 pierogi

FOR DOUGH

3½ cups flour

1 cup cold water

2 eggs

2 tablespoons Frank's® RedHot® Original Cayenne Pepper Sauce

½ teaspoon salt

FOR FILLING

1¼ cups small dice cooked chicken breast

⅔ cup finely crumbled blue cheese

1   In a large bowl, mix together all of the dough ingredients until a round, slightly sticky ball forms. Using a floured rolling pin, roll the dough out on a floured surface to ⅛ inch thick. Use a 3-inch round biscuit or cookie cutter to cut rounds in the dough.

2   Place ¾ teaspoon of chicken and 1½ teaspoons blue cheese on the bottom half of each round, leaving a ¼-inch edge free. Fold the top half of the dough over the filling and pinch shut firmly to create half-moon–shaped pierogi. Repeat until all of the rounds are filled.

3   Bring a large pot of water to a boil. Add a few pierogi at a time, being careful not to overcrowd the pot, and boil the pierogi until they float to the surface, about 5 minutes. When the pierogi float, remove them from the boiling water, using a slotted spoon, and put them on a plate. Repeat as needed until all the pierogi have been boiled.

4   Serve immediately as is or brown them in butter in a nonstick skillet over medium heat for 3–5 minutes prior to serving. Serve hot.

Atomic Wings

Hot wings are made even hotter with the addition of cayenne pepper. The flour helps give the wings an extra crispy exterior, perfect for holding onto sauce.

Makes 4 servings

24 chicken wings, separated into drums and flats

1½ tablespoons instant flour

1½ teaspoons ground cayenne pepper

salt to taste

freshly ground black pepper to taste

canola oil for frying

1½ cups **Frank's® RedHot® Hot Buffalo Wings Sauce**

1 Toss the wings with flour, cayenne pepper, salt, and pepper to taste. Set aside.

2 In a 12-inch skillet, heat 2 inches of canola oil to 350°F. Add half of the wings to the skillet. Fry until golden brown on both sides, about 10 minutes, turning as needed with tongs to make sure pieces are evenly browned. Remove to a large bowl and toss with the sauce. Repeat with the remaining wings. Toss again. Serve immediately.

Sweet Thai Wings

Tangy, sweet, and garlicky, these wings will pep up any party. Serve with additional Frank's® RedHot® Sweet Chili Sauce as a dip.

Makes 4 servings

24 chicken wings, separated into flats and drums

1 cup Frank's® RedHot® Sweet Chili Sauce

1 cup soy sauce

¼ cup rice wine vinegar

1 tablespoon minced fresh ginger

2 tablespoons minced fresh garlic

1 tablespoon spicy mustard

freshly ground black pepper to taste

1 tablespoon canola oil plus oil to grease the pan

1 Place the wings in a zip-top bag. Set aside.

2 In a small bowl, whisk together the Frank's® RedHot® Sweet Chili Sauce, soy sauce, rice wine vinegar, ginger, garlic, mustard, and pepper. Pour into the bag over the wings. Refrigerate for 30 minutes.

3 Preheat the oven to 400°F. Line a baking sheet with foil. Lightly oil the foil.

4 Drain the wings in a colander and toss them with 1 tablespoon oil in a large bowl. Arrange in a single layer and bake for 40 minutes or until fully cooked and crispy. Serve immediately.

Side Dishes

Want to flesh out the dinner plate with a spicy side? You've found the right place. Banish the boring and embrace the fire. From a surprisingly delish take on sweet potatoes to a blue cheese slaw that is as at home next to a pork chop as it is at a barbecue, there is something for everyone and every meal.

July Salad with Zesty Lime Vinaigrette

Parmesan Sweet Potatoes

Black-Eyed Peas with Ham and Turnip Greens

Smoky Hot Bacon Macaroni and Cheese

Scallion Cheddar–Hot Sauce Swirl Bread

Blue Cheese Pecan Broccoli Slaw

Mexican Street Corn Off the Cob

July Salad with Zesty Lime Vinaigrette

This recipe combines the best produce July has to offer to form a crunchy raw salad the whole family will love. For a dramatic presentation, layer the veggies in a glass bowl and serve the dressing on the side or toss in front of guests.

Makes 8 servings

4 cups fresh corn kernels

1 large English seedless cucumber, cubed

1 small zucchini, cubed

1 poblano pepper, diced

1 yellow bell pepper, diced

1 cup diced red onion

1½ cups shredded red cabbage

4 cups cherry tomatoes, halved

1 cup shredded carrot

½ cup chopped green beans

FOR VINAIGRETTE

¼ cup lime juice

3 tablespoons Frank's® RedHot® Original Cayenne Pepper Sauce

3 tablespoons olive oil

salt to taste

freshly ground black pepper to taste

1 Toss all of the salad ingredients together in a large bowl. Set aside.

2 Shake the vinaigrette ingredients in a dressing mixing container or lidded jar until well combined. Pour over the salad. Toss to evenly distribute the dressing. Serve immediately at room temperature.

Pepper Prep

To prepare peppers for a recipe, cut the top off to remove the stem. If the recipe calls for it, remove the seeds by hand. In large peppers, such as bell peppers, the seeds may be easily removed without further cutting the pepper. For smaller peppers, slice in half, then remove the seeds. Removing the seeds is mostly an aesthetic choice. Contrary to popular belief, the seeds themselves aren't actually hot; the heat comes from the oils and membrane surrounding the seeds. The heat can be slightly reduced in some peppers by cutting out the inner flesh to which the seeds are attached.

Parmesan Sweet Potatoes

This sounds like a wacky combination, but I promise, this sweet-hot-savory combination will become your new favorite side dish. Serve it with poultry or steak.

Makes 6 servings

4 large sweet potatoes, washed

2 tablespoons butter

3 tablespoons **Frank's® RedHot® Original Cayenne Pepper Sauce**

⅓ cup shredded Parmesan

salt to taste

freshly ground black pepper to taste

1 Preheat the oven to 400°F.

2 Pierce each potato in 1 or 2 places with the tip of a knife. Bake for 1 hour or until fully cooked.

3 Remove the potatoes from the oven. Peel them and discard the skin; place the pulp in a medium bowl. Add the remaining ingredients and mash until smooth. Serve immediately.

Black-Eyed Peas with Ham and Turnip Greens

Black-eyed peas and greens are both considered lucky foods and are often served on New Year's Day. However, this easy yet flavorful slow cooker dish is tasty any day of the year. Try the leftovers over cooked white rice.

Makes about 12 servings

1 pound dried black-eyed peas

6 cups ham or chicken stock

1 large onion, chopped

2 jalapeño peppers, chopped

1 stalk celery, diced

3 cloves garlic, minced

1 cup cubed ham

¼ cup Frank's® RedHot® Original Cayenne Pepper Sauce

1 tablespoon Worcestershire sauce

1 tablespoon minced fresh thyme

1 tablespoon minced fresh parsley

salt to taste

freshly ground black pepper to taste

1 pound chopped turnip greens

1 The night before you want to serve the dish, place the black-eyed peas in a 4-quart slow cooker. Fill it with water. Cover the beans and allow them to soak overnight. The following morning, drain the black-eyed peas in a colander, then return them to the slow cooker.

2 Add the stock, onion, jalapeños, celery, garlic, ham, Frank's® RedHot® Original Cayenne Pepper Sauce, Worcestershire sauce, thyme, parsley, salt, and pepper. Stir. Cook on low for 8–10 hours. One hour before serving, stir in the turnip greens and continue to cook on low for the remaining hour. Serve immediately.

Smoky Hot Bacon Macaroni and Cheese

The ultimate hot sauce lover's mac and cheese! If you aren't a fan of smoky Cheddar, use a plain sharp Cheddar or Gouda.

Makes 8 servings

1 tablespoon olive oil

1 small onion, chopped

2 cloves garlic, minced

1 (14-ounce) can diced tomatoes, drained

3 tablespoons butter

3 tablespoons flour

salt to taste

black pepper to taste

1 cup milk, at room temperature

2 cups shredded smoked Cheddar cheese

3 tablespoons **Frank's® RedHot® Original Cayenne Pepper Sauce**

4 slices thick cut bacon, cooked and crumbled

1 pound cooked macaroni

⅓ cup panko crumbs

1 Preheat the oven to 350°F.

2 In a medium skillet, heat the olive oil over medium heat. Sauté the onion and garlic until fragrant, about 2 minutes. Add the tomatoes and heat through, about 10 minutes. Set aside.

3 In a medium pan over medium heat, melt the butter. Add the flour along with salt and pepper and whisk until smooth, about 3 minutes. Add the milk and whisk together until slightly thickened, about 5–10 minutes. Whisk in the Cheddar and Frank's® RedHot® Original Cayenne Pepper Sauce.

4 Add the tomato mixture, bacon, and macaroni; stir to evenly distribute. Pour into a lightly oiled 2-quart baking dish. Top with a sprinkle of panko. Bake covered about 15 minutes, then uncover and cook until hot and bubbly, about 10–15 additional minutes. Serve immediately.

Scallion Cheddar–Hot Sauce Swirl Bread

Don't fear the yeast! This bread is worth it. Imagine, scallions folded into soft bread rolled around a filling of Frank's® RedHot® Original Cayenne Pepper Sauce and Cheddar cheese. Perfect as is or toasted and spread with a little butter.

Makes 1 loaf

¼ cup sugar

1 cup lukewarm water (about 100°F)

2 tablespoons active dry yeast

3 cups all-purpose flour

2 tablespoons canola oil

¼ teaspoon sea salt

⅓ cup diced green onions

¼ cup **Frank's® RedHot® THICK Cayenne Pepper Sauce**

¾ cup grated extra sharp Cheddar cheese

1 In a large bowl, dissolve the sugar in warm water and then stir in the yeast. Allow to sit 5 minutes.

2 Using an electric mixer with a dough hook, combine the dissolved yeast mixture on low. Slowly add the flour, oil, salt, and then green onions. Mix until a smooth, elastic ball of dough forms.

3 Place dough in a large greased bowl and cover with a damp cloth. Put the bowl in a protected space away from drafts and let the dough rise for about 45 minutes or until it doubles in size.

4 Transfer the dough to a parchment paper–lined counter. Using a floured rolling pin, roll the dough into a 14 x 8-inch rectangle about 1 inch thick. Using a pastry brush, coat the dough with an even layer of Frank's® RedHot® THICK Cayenne Pepper Sauce. Sprinkle with Cheddar to evenly coat the sauce.

5 Beginning with a short edge, roll the dough into a log. Pinch the side seam and ends closed and place in a greased loaf pan. Allow the dough to rise

for 50 minutes or until the top of the bread is about 1 inch above the top of the pan.

6 Preheat the oven to 350°F.

7 Bake loaf 30–40 minutes or until the bread is fully cooked and has a golden top crust. Remove the bread and cool on a wire rack. Serve when cool.

Pro Tip

Brush the top of the bread with 3 tablespoons of butter 15–20 minutes into the cooling time for a softer crust.

Blue Cheese Pecan Broccoli Slaw

Try this as a side to the Buffalo Chicken Burgers (page 35). Can't find broccoli slaw mix? Simply use 9 ounces of home-shredded broccoli stems and 3 ounces of shredded carrots. For extra blue cheese flavor, try Gorgonzola.

Makes 4 servings

1 (12-ounce) package broccoli slaw mix

1 small onion, finely sliced

⅓ cup halved toasted or raw pecans

⅓ cup crumbled blue cheese

FOR DRESSING

¼ cup Frank's® RedHot® Original Cayenne Pepper Sauce

¼ cup mayonnaise

1 In a medium bowl, toss together the slaw mix, onion, pecans, and cheese. Set aside.

2 In a small bowl, whisk together the dressing ingredients until smooth. Drizzle over the salad. Toss to combine and serve immediately.

Nuts About Nuts

Love nuts? Bring out their natural flavor even more by toasting them. Place nuts in a dry skillet. Toast over medium heat, stirring occasionally, for about 3 minutes or until lightly browned.

Mexican Street Corn Off the Cob

Elotes, Mexican street corn, is a tasty treat of grilled corn on the cob that is spread with a creamy sauce and sprinkled with spices and cheese. This recipe takes the corn off the cob and into a refreshing corn salad, esquites, that is as equally at home with hot dogs as it is with Mexican fare.

Makes 4 servings

6 ears fresh corn in husks

canola oil for brushing on the corn

½ cup Mexican crema

2 tablespoons mayonnaise

1½ tablespoons lime juice

1 tablespoon Frank's® RedHot® Original Cayenne Pepper Sauce

1 clove garlic, grated

½ teaspoon ground ancho chile

¼ cup chopped cilantro or flat leaf parsley

¼ cup finely crumbled cotija cheese

1 Prepare a charcoal grill according to the manufacturer's instructions.

2 Peel off the outermost layers of corn husk, leaving just a few toward the center of each ear of corn. Peel the inner husks of the corn back just enough to remove the silk while leaving the husks attached at the bottom. Discard the silk. Brush the kernels with canola oil. Pull the husks back over the corn so the kernels are covered.

3 Place the prepared ears of corn in the center of the grill. Do not close the grill cover. After 3–5 minutes, move the corn to the side of the grill and close the cover. Continue cooking the corn for another 10–15 minutes or until the kernels easily burst when poked with the tines of a fork. Remove the corn from the grill and peel off the husk.

4 Allow the corn to cool slightly, then cut the kernels off the cob. Set aside.

5 In a medium bowl, whisk together the crema, mayonnaise, lime juice, Frank's® RedHot® Original Cayenne Pepper Sauce, garlic, and ancho chile

until the mixture is uniform. Stir in the cilantro or parsley, cheese, and corn. Serve immediately.

Pro Tip
Mexican crema is similar to sour cream but has a thinner, smoother texture. Find it, along with the crumbly aged cotija cheese, in the dairy aisle of a supermarket or Mexican grocery.

Dips and Sauces

Saucy, saucy! Sauces and dips are a ridiculously easy way to add a jolt of flavor to any meal. Jazz up seafood with a zesty rémoulade or a zippy cocktail sauce. Dip amazing homemade soft pretzels in Baltimore's favorite crab dip. And don't forget: Buffalo chicken dip! This version is taking things a step further, incorporating even more Frank's® RedHot® Original Cayenne Pepper Sauce and celery to make it the best Buffalo chicken dip you'll ever make. You will be the hit of any party if you bring any of these winners!

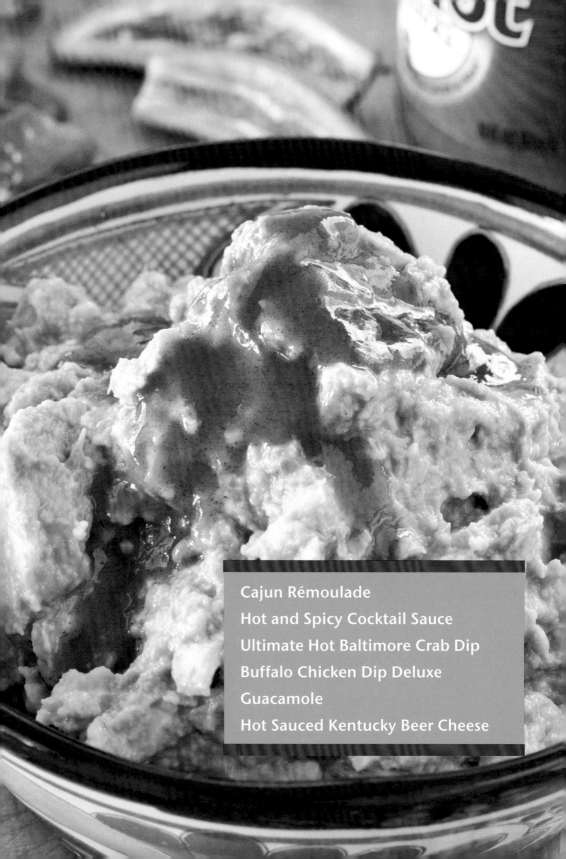

Cajun Rémoulade

Hot and Spicy Cocktail Sauce

Ultimate Hot Baltimore Crab Dip

Buffalo Chicken Dip Deluxe

Guacamole

Hot Sauced Kentucky Beer Cheese

Cajun Rémoulade

Think of rémoulade as a fancy pants version of tartar sauce. Use it on po' boys, fish and chips, shrimp, and crab cakes. It is also yummy as a dip for French fries and onion rings.

Makes about 1 cup

¾ cup mayonnaise

¼ cup small dice hot dill pickles

3 tablespoons minced fresh parsley

1 teaspoon minced fresh dill

1 teaspoon minced fresh or freeze-dried chives

½ teaspoon pickle juice (from the jar of hot dill pickles)

2 tablespoons Frank's® RedHot® Original Cayenne Pepper Sauce

1 shallot, minced

1 serrano pepper

¼ teaspoon ground hot paprika

¼ teaspoon dry mustard

1 Combine all the ingredients in a small bowl and stir to evenly distribute. Refrigerate ½ hour before serving.

Hot and Spicy Cocktail Sauce

Cocktail sauce is the perfect partner not only for shrimp; it is also divine on clam strips, crab claws, fish, burgers, and fries.

Makes about 1 cup

¾ cup tomato paste

¼ cup white vinegar

¼ cup Frank's® RedHot® Original Cayenne Pepper Sauce

¼ cup lemon juice

2 cloves garlic, peeled

1 shallot, quartered

1 tablespoon Worcestershire sauce

salt to taste

freshly ground black pepper to taste

½ cup prepared horseradish

1 Place the tomato paste, vinegar, Frank's® RedHot® Original Cayenne Pepper Sauce, lemon juice, garlic, shallot, Worcestershire sauce, salt, and pepper in a blender. Pulse until well combined. Pour into a small bowl. Stir in the horseradish. Refrigerate 1 hour prior to serving.

Ultimate Hot Baltimore Crab Dip

In Baltimore, crab is king! No party is complete without bubbling, cheesy crab dip, served with a side of crackers, chips, and sliced bread. This version kicks it up a notch with the addition of Frank's® RedHot® Original Cayenne Pepper Sauce.

Makes about 18 servings

1 cup blue crab claw meat

1 cup lump blue crab meat

1 cup cream cheese, at room temperature

¾ cup sour cream

¼ cup **Frank's® RedHot® Original Cayenne Pepper Sauce**

2½ tablespoons mayonnaise

1½ tablespoons Chesapeake Bay seasoning

½ tablespoon Worcestershire sauce

¼ teaspoon garlic powder

¼ teaspoon freshly ground black pepper

1 shallot, minced

¾ cup shredded sharp Cheddar cheese

1 Preheat the oven to 350°F.

2 In a medium bowl, stir together both crab meats, cream cheese, sour cream, Frank's® RedHot® Original Cayenne Pepper Sauce, mayonnaise, Chesapeake Bay seasoning, Worcestershire sauce, garlic powder, black pepper, and shallot until smooth.

3 Spread the mixture into an 8 x 8-inch baking dish. Sprinkle with the cheese in an even layer. Bake uncovered until the cheese is melted and the dip is warmed through, about 15 minutes. Serve immediately with crackers, chips, bread, or Soft Pretzel Sticks (recipe follows).

Soft Pretzel Sticks

Who doesn't love a soft pretzel? They are wonderful on their own but are even better as a dipper. If you can't find pretzel salt, try sesame seeds instead.

Makes 12 pretzel sticks

1 tablespoon active dry yeast	¾ cup baking soda
1½ teaspoons sugar	1 egg, beaten
1⅓ cups lukewarm water	3 tablespoons pretzel salt
4⅓ cups flour	canola oil for greasing bowl

1 In a large bowl, stir together the yeast, sugar, and warm water; let stand 3 minutes. Add the flour; mix with a stand or electric mixer with a dough hook attachment until the dough forms a smooth, elastic ball. Grease a large bowl with canola oil; place the dough in a bowl. Place in a cold oven for 50 minutes or until doubled in size.

2 Remove the bowl from the oven. Preheat oven to 425°F.

3 Gently push your fist into the dough to deflate; divide the dough into 12 pieces. Using your hands, on a floured surface, roll each piece of dough into 1-inch-thick, 10-inch-long ropes.

4 Pour baking soda into a 6- to 8-quart Dutch oven or stockpot; fill it with water to within 3 inches of the top. Stir with a whisk until the baking soda is dissolved. Heat to boiling.

5 Line a large cookie sheet with cooking parchment paper. Using tongs, dip each rope into the boiling baking soda–water mixture for 30 seconds. Place on the cookie sheet. Brush the dough with egg; sprinkle with salt. Bake 12 minutes or until golden brown. Serve warm.

Make It Even More Awesome

In Baltimore, there is a popular appetizer called the crab pretzel. It is a huge soft pretzel heaped with crab dip and tons of oozing cheese. To make it at home, make the Ultimate Hot Baltimore Crab Dip (page 109), omitting the cheese topping. Then make the pretzel dough, but instead of making it into sticks, form it into one giant pretzel. Bake as called for, then remove from the oven and spread the crab dip liberally over the top of the pretzel. Sprinkle with shredded Cheddar cheese. Return to the oven for 5 minutes to melt the cheese. Serve immediately.

Buffalo Chicken Dip Deluxe

This update on the classic dip features rotisserie chicken, crisp celery, and flavorful Gorgonzola cheese. Use a stand mixer with a paddle attachment to mix the dip even more quickly than by hand.

Makes 12 to 15 servings

2 cups finely diced rotisserie chicken breast

⅓ cup finely diced onion

⅓ cup finely diced celery

1 cup Neufchâtel cheese (⅓-less-fat cream cheese), at room temperature

⅔ cup sour cream

¾ cup Frank's® RedHot® Original Cayenne Pepper Sauce

¾ cup crumbled Gorgonzola cheese

1 In a large bowl, use a large spoon to stir together all the ingredients until evenly distributed. Refrigerate at least 1 hour prior to serving.

Do-It-Yourself Chicken

Don't have rotisserie chicken on hand? Substitute cubed poached chicken breast. Place 2 bone-in chicken breasts in a stockpot filled with enough water to cover the chicken. Add a bay leaf, half an onion, 2 cloves garlic, a stalk of celery, and a carrot. Bring to a boil, then reduce to a simmer for 20 minutes or until the chicken is cooked through. Allow to cool, then remove from the bone and dice.

Guacamole

Sure, you can serve this game day favorite with chips, but why not branch out and use it in a burrito or taco or as a burger topper?

Makes about 10 servings

1 medium tomato, cubed

4 avocados, peeled and pitted

3 tablespoons lime juice

3 tablespoons Frank's® RedHot® Original Cayenne Pepper Sauce or Frank's® RedHot® Chile N' Lime™ Hot Sauce

1 shallot, minced

2 serrano peppers, minced

⅛ cup cilantro, minced

⅛ cup flat leaf parsley, minced

1 teaspoon garlic powder

freshly ground black pepper to taste

1 Place the tomato in the middle of a paper towel and squeeze to remove the juices. Set aside.

2 In medium bowl, use a potato masher to mash the avocados to desired constancy. Add the lime juice and Frank's® RedHot® Original Cayenne Pepper Sauce or Frank's® RedHot® Chile N' Lime™ Hot Sauce. Stir to combine.

3 Add all the other ingredients, stirring to evenly distribute. Cover the mixture with plastic wrap, pressing it slightly into the guacamole to prevent oxidation, and chill for ½ hour prior to serving.

Guacamole: Did You Know?

• Guacamole was first made by the Aztecs in Mexico.

• Avocados were once called "alligator pears" in English-speaking countries, and guacamole was referred to as "salad of alligator pear" in cookbooks.

• A *molcajete*, the mortar and pestle in which guacamole traditionally is made, is carved out of a single block of volcanic rock.

Hot Sauced Kentucky Beer Cheese

Rarely seen outside of Kentucky, this smooth and creamy spread is perfect for game day or any time! Try it stuffed into celery sticks, spread on crackers, or as a dip for pretzels.

Makes about 2½ cups

1 pound brick extra sharp white Cheddar cheese, shredded

1 clove garlic, chopped

1 shallot, quartered

2 teaspoons Worcestershire sauce

1 teaspoon ground mustard

½ teaspoon freshly ground black pepper

½ teaspoon ground chipotle pepper

½ cup amber ale

¼ cup Frank's® RedHot® Original Cayenne Pepper Sauce

1 Place the cheese, garlic, shallot, Worcestershire sauce, and spices into a food processor fitted with the blade attachment. Cover and begin to process. While the food processor is running, slowly stream in the beer, then the Frank's® RedHot® Original Cayenne Pepper Sauce. Continue to process until smooth.

2 Use a spatula to scrape the mixture into a medium bowl. Cover and refrigerate at least 2 hours and up to overnight before serving.

Hot and Sweet

I know what you are thinking. Um, Frank's® RedHot® Original Cayenne Pepper Sauce in... dessert? Oh, yes! Not only can you do it, it is fabulous! It turns out that the fiery hotness pairs perfectly with the sweetness. Try breaking up Hot Nuts Brittle over homemade Honeyed Beer–Hot Sauce Ice Cream. You read that correctly, hot sauce ice cream. Hot sauce ice cream! If that isn't enough to entice you, cool off with a Mexican ice pop or spice-ify those peaches in an amazing crumble. You can take the heat straight from breakfast to dessert.

Spiced Sweet Potato Pie with Gingersnap Pecan Crust

Hot Nuts Brittle

Mango Hot Paletas

Honeyed Beer–Hot Sauce Ice Cream

Cinnamon Cayenne Buns with Frank's® RedHot® Original Cayenne Pepper Sauce Cream Cheese Frosting

Sugar and Spice (and Everything Nice) Peach Crumble

Spiced Sweet Potato Pie with Gingersnap Pecan Crust

Personally, my favorite way to eat sweet potatoes is in pie form. This pie provides a jolt of heat in the creamy, sweet filling, making it a pie worthy of royalty. The pie crust is special too; it adds a ton of gingersnap and pecan flavor. So much better than plain old pie crust.

Makes about 12 servings

FOR PIE CRUST

1½ cups coarse Hot Gingersnap cookie crumbs (from approximately 20 cookies) (recipe follows)

½ cup ground roasted or raw pecans

5 tablespoons butter, melted

FOR PIE FILLING

3 cups mashed, roasted sweet potato

3 eggs

2 tablespoons Frank's® RedHot® Original Cayenne Pepper Sauce

3 tablespoons butter, melted and cooled

10 tablespoons evaporated milk

¼ cup firmly packed dark brown sugar

½ teaspoon cinnamon

1 teaspoon ground ginger

½ teaspoon ground allspice

¼ teaspoon ground cloves

1   Preheat the oven to 350°F.

2   To make the pie crust, whisk together the cookie crumbs and pecans in a medium bowl. Drizzle with melted butter. Stir with a fork until it looks like damp sand. Press into the bottom and sides of a pie tin in an even layer. Bake 10 minutes. Remove to a wire rack to cool.

3   To make the filling, place all the ingredients in a large bowl. Mix together, using an electric mixer, until all the ingredients are well incorporated and the mixture is fairly smooth.

4 Pour into the prepared pie crust. Bake for 60 minutes or until the pie is set and no longer shiny.

5 Cool completely on a wire rack. Serve when cool.

Pro Tips

- Use a food processor or powerful mixer to grind the cookies into crumbs. Simply pulse until the desired texture is reached and no large chunks remain.

- Wash the potatoes, pierce each potato in 1 or 2 places with the tip of a knife, and then roast the potatoes for 1 hour at 400°F or until soft. Scoop the flesh out and discard the skin. Allow the potatoes to cool completely, then mash. This can be done the night before you'd like to make the pie.

- Use the flat bottom of a measuring cup to smooth and flatten the crumbs into the bottom and sides of the pie tin.

Hot Gingersnaps

Be a baking superstar and use these cookies to make the crumbs for the Gingersnap Pecan Crust for the Spiced Sweet Potato Pie (previous recipe). The cookies (and crust!) can be made the day before you'd like to make the pie.

Makes about 2 dozen cookies

⅔ cup demerara sugar

½ cup butter, softened

⅔ cup sugar

1 egg

3 tablespoons molasses

1½ cups flour

3 teaspoons ground ginger

¾ teaspoon ground cinnamon

¾ teaspoon ground cayenne pepper

1 teaspoon baking powder

¼ teaspoon salt

1 Preheat the oven to 350°F. Line 2 cookie sheets with parchment paper. Pour the demerara sugar in a shallow bowl. Set aside.

2 In a large bowl, with an electric mixer, cream together the butter and sugar. Add the egg and molasses and mix well. In a separate medium bowl, whisk together the flour, ginger, cinnamon, cayenne, baking powder, and salt. Slowly add it to the butter and sugar mixture while the mixer is running. Mix to thoroughly combine.

3 Using the palms of your hands, roll the dough into 1-inch balls. Roll the balls in the demerara sugar to coat. Place the cookies 2 inches apart on the cookie sheets. Flatten each cookie slightly with the heel of your hand or a spatula.

4 Bake 8–12 minutes or until set and the bottoms are golden. Cool completely on a wire rack, then serve.

Pro Tip

Demerara sugar, a coarse raw cane brown sugar, is also known as turbinado sugar. If unavailable, omit it from the recipe or use coarse sanding sugar.

Hot Nuts Brittle

Sweet and spicy, this new brittle is sure to please! Try it as is or, better yet, sprinkle over vanilla ice cream for a sundae that sizzles. Caution: The sugar mixture will be very hot. This recipe should be made with care, by adults only.

Makes 8 to 10 servings

1½ cups slivered almonds

1 cup sugar

½ cup light corn syrup

8 tablespoons (1 stick) butter, cubed

2 tablespoons Frank's® RedHot® Original Cayenne Pepper Sauce

½ teaspoon baking soda

1 Line a baking sheet with parchment paper. Set aside.

2 Place the almonds in a medium-sized dry skillet. Toast the almonds over medium heat, stirring occasionally, about 3 minutes. Remove the pan from the heat but keep the almonds in the pan.

3 In a medium saucepan, bring the sugar, corn syrup, butter, and Frank's® RedHot® Original Cayenne Pepper Sauce to a boil. Continue to cook, stirring occasionally, for 10 minutes or until the mixture darkens and a dollop of the mixture dropped into a cup of cold water hardens instantly. Stir in the baking soda. Fold in the almonds. Immediately pour the mixture onto the lined baking sheet and use a spoon to create a layer between ⅛ and ¼ inch thick. Allow to cool completely. Break into bite-sized pieces. Serve immediately.

Quick Variations

• Use unsalted peanuts, skinned hazelnuts, or pecans in place of the slivered almonds.

• Make it extra spicy: Add ¼ teaspoon ground cayenne to the mixture when you add the nuts.

• Dip the bottom of each piece in melted chocolate. Cool chocolate side up on a wire rack with a baking sheet underneath to catch drips.

Mango Hot Paletas

Mango on a stick doused with chile powder and lime is a favorite street snack in Mexico, as are paletas, Mexican ice pops. Combine the two into one tasty treat with these spicy sweet frozen pops.

Makes about 6 ice pops

3 cups cubed fresh mango

⅔ cup lime juice

1½ tablespoons Frank's® RedHot® Original Cayenne Pepper Sauce

1 tablespoon sugar

½ teaspoon lime zest

1   Place all the ingredients in a blender and pulse until almost smooth. Divide evenly into ice pop molds, leaving a ¼-inch headspace. Seal and freeze until solid, about 4 hours. Serve immediately or within 6 months (if kept frozen).

Honeyed Beer–Hot Sauce Ice Cream

The seemingly disparate ingredients of honey, Frank's® RedHot® Original Cayenne Pepper Sauce, and beer come together to make a decadent ice cream that any ice cream lover will adore.

Makes about 1 pint

4 tablespoons clover honey

4 tablespoons Frank's® RedHot® Original Cayenne Pepper Sauce

1½ cups ale

1 cup heavy cream

1½ cups whole milk

½ cup sugar, divided for use

4 egg yolks

1 Whisk together the honey, Frank's® RedHot® Original Cayenne Pepper Sauce, and ale in a 2-quart saucepan. Cook over medium heat until the mixture is reduced to ½ cup, about 15 minutes. Set aside.

2 In a large pot over medium heat, whisk together the cream, milk, and ¼ cup sugar until the sugar dissolves and the mixture almost boils, about 2–3 minutes.

3 Meanwhile, in a separate medium bowl or bowl of a stand mixer, use a mixer with a whisk attachment to whisk together the remaining sugar and egg yolks until it is yellow and creamy, about 1–2 minutes. Add about ½ cup of the cream mixture into the egg mixture and whisk to combine.

4 Pour the egg and cream mixture into the cream mixture on the stove. Add the beer mixture and cook, stirring occasionally, for about 8 minutes or until the mixture coats the back of a spoon. Allow to cool on the counter for 25–30 minutes. Strain the mixture through a fine mesh sieve, whisking the mixture through to remove any solids, into a medium bowl. Refrigerate overnight.

5 Pour through a fine mesh sieve into an ice cream maker and churn, following the manufacturer's instructions, until cold and set. Eat immediately or place in a freezer-safe container and freeze until solid.

Cinnamon Cayenne Buns with Frank's® RedHot® Original Cayenne Pepper Sauce Cream Cheese Frosting

Finally, the cinnamon bun for which the hot sauce lover has been waiting. I took a traditional cinnamon recipe, spiked it with cayenne pepper, and then made a decadent Frank's® RedHot® Original Cayenne Pepper Sauce cream cheese frosting. It is as equally at home at breakfast as it is at dessert. Or as a midday snack!

Makes 9 buns

FOR DOUGH
½ cup butter, cubed

1¼ cups milk

1 tablespoon active dry yeast

1 tablespoon sugar

½ cup firmly packed dark brown sugar

1 egg, beaten

1 teaspoon salt

4 cups flour

FOR FILLING
½ cup butter, at room temperature

1¼ cups firmly packed dark brown sugar

2 tablespoons cinnamon

½ teaspoon ground cayenne pepper

FOR ICING
6 tablespoons cream cheese, softened

3 tablespoons butter, softened

1½ cups confectioners' sugar

1 teaspoon Frank's® RedHot® Original Cayenne Pepper Sauce

TO MAKE THE DOUGH

1 In a small saucepan over medium heat, melt the butter. Allow to cool 5 minutes. Return to the heat and whisk in the milk. Milk burns easily, so be careful not to overheat it and burn it. Simmer until it reaches 100°F. Pour into a large bowl. Sprinkle with the yeast and sugar. Allow to sit 5 minutes.

2 Using an electric mixer with a dough hook, combine the dissolved yeast and the butter mixture on low. Slowly add the brown sugar, then the egg. Add the salt and 2 cups of flour on low, mixing until well incorporated. Slowly mix in the remaining 2 cups of flour. The mixture should become a slightly sticky but uniform dough at this time.

3 Scrape out the dough onto a floured countertop. Knead the dough until it doesn't stick to your hands, adding small amounts of flour (up to ½ cup) as needed. Place in a large greased bowl. Cover with a damp cloth and let rise for about 45 minutes or until it doubles in size.

4 Remove the dough from the bowl and place on a floured counter. Using a floured rolling pin, roll out in a 12 by 24-inch rectangle. The dough should be about 1 inch thick.

TO MAKE THE FILLING

1 In a small bowl, whisk the butter until smooth and fluffy. Using an icing spatula, spread the whipped butter over the dough. In small bowl, whisk together the brown sugar, cinnamon, and cayenne for the filling. Sprinkle evenly over the buttered dough. Roll the dough into a tight log. Cut into 1-inch-thick slices. Place in 2 ungreased 9-inch round cake pans, forming a circle with one roll in the middle. Allow to rise about ½ hour, until they are about level with the top of the cake pan.

2 Preheat the oven to 350°F.

3 Bake the rolls for 15–20 minutes, until fully cooked. Remove to a wire rack and cool 5 minutes in the pan, then invert onto a plate.

4 Whisk together the icing ingredients until smooth. Spread on slightly warm buns. Serve immediately.

Sugar and Spice (and Everything Nice) Peach Crumble

An old-fashioned classic updated with the addition of Frank's® RedHot® Original Cayenne Pepper Sauce. It is sure to be a new favorite. Try it with a scoop of cooling vanilla ice cream. If fresh peaches are not in season, substitute 2 pounds defrosted, frozen peeled peach slices.

Makes about 9 servings

FOR TOPPING

⅓ cup old fashioned rolled oats

⅔ cup flour

⅓ cup firmly packed dark brown sugar

½ teaspoon cinnamon

¼ teaspoon ground cayenne pepper

¼ teaspoon ground allspice

¼ cup (4 tablespoons) butter, melted

FOR FILLING

2 pounds peeled peach slices

½ cup firmly packed dark brown sugar

1 teaspoon cornstarch

⅓ cup flour

2 tablespoons lemon juice

2 tablespoons Frank's® RedHot® THICK Cayenne Pepper Sauce

1 Preheat the oven to 375°F. Lightly grease or spray with nonstick baking spray an 8 x 8-inch baking pan. Set aside.

2 In a small bowl, whisk together the oats, flour, dark brown sugar, cinnamon, cayenne, and allspice. Drizzle with melted butter. Mix with a fork until crumbs form and the mixture looks damp. Set aside.

3 In a medium bowl, stir together all of the filling ingredients until the flour is dissolved and the peach slices are well coated. Pour the filling into the prepared pan. Top with an even layer of the topping. Bake 45 minutes or until bubbly and heated through. Serve immediately.

Common Conversions

1 gallon = 4 quarts = 8 pints = 16 cups = 128 fluid ounces = 3.8 liters

1 quart = 2 pints = 4 cups = 32 ounces = .95 liter

1 pint = 2 cups = 16 ounces = 480 ml

1 cup = 8 ounces = 240 ml

¼ cup = 4 tablespoons = 12 teaspoons = 2 ounces = 60 ml

Temperature Conversions

Fahrenheit (°F)	Celsius (°C)
200°F	95°C
225°F	110°C
250°F	120°C
275°F	135°C
300°F	150°C
325°F	165°C
350°F	175°C
375°F	190°C
400°F	200°C
425°F	220°C
450°F	230°C
475°F	245°C

Volume Conversions

U.S.	U.S. equivalent	Metric
1 tablespoon (3 teaspoons)	½ fluid ounce	15 milliliters
¼ cup	2 fluid ounces	60 milliliters
⅓ cup	3 fluid ounces	90 milliliters
½ cup	4 fluid ounces	120 milliliters
⅔ cup	5 fluid ounces	150 milliliters
¾ cup	6 fluid ounces	180 milliliters
1 cup	8 fluid ounces	240 milliliters
2 cups	16 fluid ounces	480 milliliters

Weight Conversions

U.S.	Metric
½ ounce	15 grams
1 ounce	30 grams
2 ounces	60 grams
¼ pound	115 grams
⅓ pound	150 grams
½ pound	225 grams
¾ pound	350 grams
1 pound	450 grams

Index

About the Author

Rachel Rappaport is an award-winning recipe developer, cookbook author, and food blogger. Her blog, Coconut & Lime (www.coconutand lime.com), features more than 1,600 of her original recipes and was named one of the top fifty food blogs in the world by MSN's Delish.com. Her work has been featured by NPR, the *Washington Post*, the *LA Times*, the *Baltimore Sun*, and Fox News. She has appeared on several news, radio, and web shows demonstrating recipes and offering commentary.

Rachel is the author of *The Everything Healthy Slow Cooker Cookbook*, *The Everything Whole Foods Cookbook*, *The Big Book of Slow Cooker Recipes*, and *The Big Book of Vegetarian Recipes*. Rachel lives in Baltimore, Maryland.